Life Lessons

Other Books by Don Reid

Heroes and Outlaws of the Bible
Sunday Morning Memories
You Know It's Christmas When... (with Debo Reid and
　　Langdon Reid)
Random Memories (with Harold Reid)
O Little Town
One Lane Bridge
The Mulligans of Mt. Jefferson
Half and Half
The Music of The Statler Brothers: An Anthology

DonReid.net
TheStatlerBrothers.com

Life Lessons

Don Reid

MERCER UNIVERSITY PRESS
Macon, Georgia
2021

MUP/ H1007

© 2021 by REID PARTNERSHIP, LLC

Published by Mercer University Press
1501 Mercer University Drive
Macon, Georgia 31207
All rights reserved

25 24 23 22 21   5 4 3 2 1

Books published by Mercer University Press are printed on acid-free paper that meets the requirements of the American National Standard for Information Sciences—Permanence of Paper for Printed Library Materials.

Printed and bound in the United States.

This book is set in Adobe Caslon Pro.

Cover/jacket design by Burt&Burt.

ISBN 978-0-88146-796-3
Cataloging-in-Publication Data is available from the Library of Congress

To four very special people in my life,

my grandchildren,

CAROLINE, SELA, DAVIS, and ADRA.

If just one story, in years to come, means something special

to any one of you, then this book will have been

worthwhile.

Love you dearly,

Poppy

MERCER UNIVERSITY PRESS

Endowed by

TOM WATSON BROWN
and
THE WATSON-BROWN FOUNDATION, INC.

Contents

ix

Preface

I have been teaching an adult Sunday school class at my home church of Olivet Presbyterian for more than thirty-five years. (I should edit that statement a bit and say I have "moderated" a class for that period of time, because I usually come out of there every week with more than I put into it.) It has been, and is, a life experience I would never want to be without. There in the Friendship Class, we talk about every subject imaginable, from the Bible to current events to feelings to life problems to what makes us happy and sad to what is important to each of us and then back again to the Bible. (All biblical quotes are from the King James Version [KJV] or the New International Version [NIV].) We have a wonderful, eclectic group with a large age range that gives us all a good perspective on any topic that arises. I have never used a standard lesson book for these topics but have always relied on what was on my mind and in my heart each week to spark the research and conversation.

This pleasant and amiable format was rudely interrupted in March of 2020 when the COVID-19 pandemic scare closed down the churches and sent us all to Facebook streaming for our morning services. The Sunday school hour went dark, and there were no more friendly discussions sitting around in our circle, no more exchanging of views, no more drinking coffee and laughing together, no more listening to one another's troubles and praying in person for personal solutions. At this new and unusual turn, I took the lead to offer something via email each Saturday night to all the class members and a few good friends added along the way. I wrote a mini-version of what I would have normally prepared, and had it in their inbox for Sunday morning. Sometimes it was a Bible story we could all relate to, and sometimes it was a remembrance with a message I hoped would find a place for them to fit into their upcoming week. And that's what I'm hoping you'll find in the pages ahead. Something that will fulfill, explain, and enlighten—even calm, heal, and entertain.

Scattered throughout these pages are twelve chapters about the Apostle Peter. I chose him as a particular study because his life is so relatable to our own. Peter had his highs and lows, his embarrassments, his days when his faith was stronger than it was on other days, his stumbling blocks, and his shining moments. I think he's a wonderful example for any of us who find ourselves dealing with this thing called human nature.

I've tweaked and done little rewrites on a few of these random and sundry topics, but in essence, I speak to you here as I speak to the class each week. Informally, friendly, and without favoritism to political views or social issues or attitudes that tend to divide. I want the message to be for everyone who cares and hopefully believes. These Life Lessons, as I tend to call them, are just thoughts and words I have been given, much like the ones you are given for each situation that arises in your daily living. Use them, share them, and add to them in your own personal way.

My sincere wish is that you find something in each of these chapters that makes you pause, think, and want to read the next one.

May every lesson in our lives be a blessing,

Don

Passing It On

I got caught up in something today. Something good that many of you have probably experienced. I was out running errands, listening to Bill Gaither's *Homecoming* radio show around lunch time, and whipped into a McDonald's drive-thru. As I'm pulling up to the window with money in hand, the smiling girl said, "The car in front of you has paid your check." I was stunned and unable to see around the corner to see who it might have been. But in the only way I knew how to say thank you, I said to the young lady, "That was terribly nice. Then I'll pay for whoever is behind me." I did, and all the time I was sitting in the parking lot eating my Big Mac and fries, I had a nice feeling for what had happened to me and what I had just done. I was truly caught up in the moment and I smiled all the way through lunch.

I still have no idea who was in front of me or behind me, and I suppose I never will. I have never been caught in the middle of one of these random acts of kindness. I've been at the front but never in the center, and it made me wonder just how long the stream of "passing it on" might have continued. There is probably a statistic somewhere on the internet that tells us that the record-setting number of cars is fifteen or forty-two or 106. Everything else can be found out there in cyberworld, and I'm sure this can be, too. But the point is not how long it continued but that it happened at all.

There are so many good-hearted, loving folks out there who show their kindness in so many varied ways. Not everybody has the ability to walk up to someone and ask if they would like to have a prayer with them. And many people would be immediately turned off if someone did this to them. Not everybody is comfortable walking up and offering financial help to someone who looks like they might need it. You never know who might be offended by this. Many may not even be comfortable inviting a stranger to their church. Many might want to befriend someone in need by just offering an ear but don't know how best to approach the situation. So, passing it on in a drive-thru is about as good a way as any. It says so much.

> *Be ye kind one to another, tenderhearted,*
> *forgiving one another*
> —Ephesians 4:32

When we were kids growing up, our home was full of little things my sister and brother and I made at school or Bible school or even around the house. I remember a little wooden plaque with this Bible verse printed on it that brother Harold had made and painted the letters in bright green: BE YE KIND. It sat on the mantle in the dining room for many, many years. I saw it every day. As a kid, I didn't always act on it, but it reminded me every day that I should. After all these years it has had a remaining influence on me. It takes no more effort to be kind than it does to be short or curt. And the effect it has on the people around you will be obvious. Hey, they may even say something nice about you after you walk away. I saw written on a sweatshirt the other day: "In a world where you can be anything...be kind."

The message is there for us all. We don't have to have any tools of the trade to express ourselves. We don't have to have any particular talent for conversation. We don't have to have a winning personality. We can just show some kindness at every turn and it will make the old heart feel better all day long. Even if it's in a drive-thru at McDonald's.

Make somebody smile this week. God Bless you.

Answers

The older I get, the more I realize I don't know. And surprisingly, that doesn't bother me in the least. There was a time—and every one of you will attest to this to some degree—when it seemed important to have an answer to every question that arose. You felt an obligation to tackle and solve whatever was put before you. It was like an obstacle course of life and you didn't want to admit there were some things you couldn't win. "What has changed?" I ask myself. And the answer is simple. *I* have.

A number of years ago there was a popular saying going around: *Let go and let God.* Like everything else in our disposable society of life, it went out of style and you don't hear it much anymore. But that doesn't mean it has lost any of its power. I still like it. Of course, I still like button-down collars and khakis, so there you go.

All of our lives, from the day we were born, it is instilled in us that it is our job to take care of our families at all cost. To raise our children and make all decisions that are good for them. To provide for their needs. Put food on the table. Put clothes on their backs. Buy insurance—car, life, health care. Buy a home. Provide college. Men and women alike are taught, and it is drilled into us, that we are responsible for our own welfare and the well-being of all those legally dependent upon us. And that, my friends, is the American way. If we can't do this, then we have failed in the eyes of all those around us. We have let down those we love and those who look up to and love us. If our shoulders aren't big enough and strong enough to carry the weight, then we just might as well pack it all in and roll over and go back to sleep. We're taught not to whine, and we're often embarrassed to ask for help. We promise ourselves to try harder the next time and the next and the next.

And then...as Christians, we have to realize and admit that we *can't* do it all. We can't even do a little bit of it. We must have God and we must lean on him for everything. Even our very next breath. We need him for all decisions, big and small. There was a great song on the subject a few years ago that says it as good as can be said:

> *I thought I could do a lot on my own*
> *I thought I could make it all alone*
> *I thought of myself as a mighty big man*
> *But, Lord, I can't even walk without you holding*
>   *my hand*
> "I Can't Even Walk (Without You Holding My Hand)"
>   —Pastor Colbert and Joyce Croft

And that is when you realize you don't have all the answers and you're not ashamed to admit it. You get to that stage and that age, and you are glad to turn it all over to someone who can get the job done. All my life I have been doing public appearances, speaking engagements, and pulpit supply, and there is a little prayer I say to myself every time, just before I step up to face an audience or a congregation or any gathering. I say:

Lord, I have prepared to the best of my ability. It is now in Your hands, as it always is. Please help it mean something to someone and please keep me from making a fool of myself. Amen.

Folks ask me all the time if I have ever gotten nervous in front of a crowd. Never. It's in his hands, not mine. He's got the answers, not me.

The mountain's too high, the valley's too wide
But down on my knees, I learned to stand
And, Lord, I can't even walk without
    you holding my hand

Bro James

I remember as a kid hearing my dad say that someone "couldn't see the forest for the trees." I had to hear that quite a few times before I finally figured out just exactly what he meant. If you are too close to a situation, you can only see a few trees. It isn't until you back up and away from them a little that you can see the big picture and see the actual forest—see what it looks like and how big it really is. Wow! That was quite a revelation for a little ole kid no smarter than I was or am.

Throughout history, we have had quite a few famous brothers. Take the James brothers, Frank and Jesse, of the Wild West. The Wright brothers, Wilbur and Orville, of aeronautics acclaim. The Kennedy brothers, Jack, Bobby, and Ted, of mid-twentieth-century politics. Then add the disciple brothers in the Bible: Peter and Andrew, James and John, Matthew and James, the son of Alphaeus. These were all blood and commitment relationships. They thought alike and dedicated themselves to the same causes and beliefs. There were many more we could cite, but the most interesting sibling brotherhood to me has always been Jesus and his brother James, who was *not* one of the Twelve. They did *not* share views and values and religion. Well, not until later in life for one of them.

These two brothers, sons of Joseph and Mary, along with siblings Joseph, Judas, Simon, and some sisters, grew up together in Nazareth. Maybe Jesus and James shared a room growing up, the way brothers and sisters often do. Maybe they teased one another, had nicknames for one another, had boyhood secrets, went on little adventures together. If so, that all changed in adulthood because early in Jesus' ministry, his family, not understanding his actions and words, came to rescue him from himself, and said, "He is out of his mind." Very likely, James was a part of this family intervention. The book of John tells us clearly in one powerful and shocking sentence, "Even his own brothers did not believe in him."

> *A prophet is not without honor except in his hometown, among his relatives, and in his household.*
> —Mark 6:4 (words of Jesus)

So, Jesus knew how his family felt about him, and it couldn't have been an easy pill to swallow. But then there came that time when brother James saw the light, when he came to believe in his heart that the boy he had grown up with and played with and worked with as a young man was truly the Son of God. And that time was the Resurrection.

Brother James became not just a believer, but within ten years after Jesus' death, became the acknowledged leader of the Christian church in Jerusalem. He was a respected friend of the Apostle Paul in life and a martyr of his brother's ministry in death. Often called James the Just, James the First Bishop of Jerusalem, and James the Brother of the Lord, though not biblical, we are told he was thrown from the top of the temple, then clubbed and beaten to death for his Christian belief.

Early on, James was too close to the trees to see the forest but when he stepped back for a better look, he not only saw the forest, he saw the Cross.

When I sit on our patio in the summer evenings, reading until dark, I have a most serene and relaxing view looking northeast. Among so many tall treetops, I can see the lone steeple from a neighborhood church sticking up through the greenery. It has a cross on top of it, and it's a pleasant feeling watching the day end and seeing that steeple glisten in the last glow of sunlight. Like brother James, I can see the forest and the Cross at the same time, and I have to tell you, it's a pretty peaceful feeling.

Come near to God and he will come near to you.
—James 4:8

May your week be full of the Spirit and your heart full of love.

Portrait of a Church

A beautiful old Baptist church in Wakefield, Massachusetts, started having its problems about a year and a half before COVID-19 started giving all our churches such headaches. The First Baptist Church, a large white building at 1 Church Street, stood since 1872, serving the city and Christian families for 146 years. But the world changed for all those members the night of October 23, 2018, when their place of worship was destroyed by fire.

A storm blew up, with heavy winds and rain and flashing lightning. And it was a bolt of lightning that hit the steeple that began all their problems. More than one hundred firefighters rushed to the scene, but to no avail. A church meeting was going on inside at the time, and thankfully everyone escaped without injury, but so much damage was done to the stately old building that what the fire didn't get, the bulldozers had to finish. But God left a sign for all these loyal congregants that just could not go unnoticed by anyone with any amount of faith. There, buried among the ashes where nothing else was saved, they found a portrait of Christ, untouched and unharmed. No fire damage. No smoke damage. No water damage. Just a large, stunning, framed, color picture of Jesus. You've seen it many times. A full-length picture of him in a white robe with both hands stretched out toward us.

A neighboring church gave this church family a place to worship while they began their rebuilding program. But the mystery of the portrait still lingered with the members. What did it mean, and what should they do with it? They decided to give it to a former pastor they all admired as a gift. A beautiful sign from God and a beautiful gesture to honor an old friend and shepherd.

This is a group of Christians with their heads on straight, looking for no sensationalism, needing no special attention, and feeling no extraordinary proof of the beliefs they have maintained all their lives. The storm took their building, God left them a sign, and they have moved on in their walk of faith.

Was this really a sign from God? Has God ever given you a sign? Has something miraculous ever happened that you just knew came directly from him? Are we tuned in enough to recognize all the signs God might give us? When we pray for guidance in making decisions and choices, we don't expect to be answered by the voice of God. No, we expect to be answered by signs, some so subtle they could get past us in everyday living.

Some of God's obvious and blatant signs are easy to see and understand. We were given the sign of the rainbow and then were told what it meant—that the world would never be destroyed again by water. Moses was given three signs over in the book of Exodus when (1) God turned his staff into a snake, (2) when God told him to put his hand inside his coat, after which it turned snow white with leprosy before turning back to normal, and (3) when God told him to take water from the Nile, pour it on the ground, and it would become blood. God gave Gideon the signs he asked for and certainly gave Paul a life-changing sign on the Damascus road.

True, we may never see anything as miraculous and as obvious as these, but if we keep our eyes open and our hearts in the right place, we will see proof of God's interaction in our lives every day we live. It might be something as simple as the weather that takes a turn for the better and makes an event possible that at first looked threatening. Or a fever that breaks with the morning that makes the sun shine a little brighter that day. Or a phone call just when you needed to talk to that person. Or an unexpected kindness that came at a time when your spirits needed lifting.

I received a sign, and it was right there at my church, Olivet, on a Sunday morning in June on the old ballfield behind our church. After twelve weeks of cancellations due to COVID-19, our faithful and loving congregation came together in the sweet morning sun in the grassy field and worshipped the way we had been longing to for the past three months. The faces I had been wanting to see, the families I had missed being with, the friendly greetings and the passing conversations. We couldn't shake hands or hug, but we didn't need to. God had his arms around all of us at the same time, and the world was right again. All summer long we would enjoy his outdoor beauty while listening to his Word. It's a sign that he is still in charge and still gives us refuge from all the things that keep us from turning on the news every day.

To him be the glory. There is peace in God's will.

What a Leader Looks Like

This is the first of the chapters on Peter I mentioned in the preface. During the Easter season, I decided to look not just to the Scriptures and life experiences, but to a particular icon of the New Testament who teaches and instructs with his very lifestyle. The perfect person to personify the joys and hardships of being faithful is the much-loved disciple Peter. In twelve separate episodes, spread throughout this book, we'll look at his life and his relationship with Jesus and his struggles with his faith. I may not bring anything new to the table you don't already know, but something in this study may remind you of small facts that sometimes get lost in the cobwebs of time, somewhere in the recesses of our minds. So often I have reread stories in the Bible, and without fail I pick up something new each time. Something resonates that didn't stick with me the other times before. I hope there is something in each one of these that may spark a little interest and inspiration. So, let's begin our first look at this man called Peter.

Andrew, usually thought to be the first disciple, was the one who brought his brother, Peter, to Jesus. Peter was a strong-willed, impulsive, and even brash kind of guy at times. He and Andrew were from the ancient village of Bethsaida, as was the Apostle Philip. Jesus would subsequently perform a couple of miracles just outside of their hometown. He would give a blind man sight and feed the five thousand there.

Peter, a fisherman by trade, was also a born leader. In no time, he became the head spokesman for the twelve disciples. Scripture shows us he spoke up often, asking Jesus pertinent questions that allowed Jesus such perfect teaching moments. Peter would ask things such as, "Master, what does that parable mean?" and "Lord, how many times should I forgive my brother?" And it was Peter who had the fortitude and courage to actually say to Jesus, "Look, Rabbi, the fig tree you cursed has withered" after Jesus had put a curse on a tree in apparent anger.

A spot-on example of just how rash and forward ole Peter could be is seen when Jesus is telling the Twelve how he would have to go to Jerusalem and suffer at the hands of the elders and chief priests and then be killed and raised from the dead. Peter actually caught hold of Jesus, took him aside, and scolded him and lectured him, saying, "No, Master, this can never happen to you!" Can you imagine putting hands on Jesus and refuting his words? But Peter did. Out of love and protection, understand, but still it was of such force and determination that Jesus came back at him with, "Get thee behind me, Satan." This was because Satan, not God, was at that moment speaking through Peter.

But as if to show the loving and forgiving nature of the Christ, just six days later, Jesus chose Peter as one of the three to accompany him up the mountain to witness one of the most fantastic and amazing sights in all history, the Transfiguration.

This is the kind of Lord Peter was chosen to serve. And the same can be said for us. In future chapters, as we get to look at Peter and his purpose a little closer, we may even see our own with a little more understanding. We'll see how weak and wrong and faithless a believer can be one moment and how quickly God can forgive the next. God promises to fully forgive; it's usually we who have the problem of forgiving ourselves.

QUESTION FOR THOUGHT

Who were the three disciples who saw the Transfiguration and on what mountain did it take place?

ANSWER

Peter, James, and John. The name of the mountain is never stated in the Scriptures, but historians believe it was either Mount Tabor or Mount Hermon.

A Heart of Wisdom

Most people think they have or had the best and most loving mother that ever walked the earth. Yet I have known way too many who think the very opposite of their maternal influences. I, thankfully, fall in the category of the former. I could write a story every week about my mother—about the things she said, things she did, her love, her compassion, her thoughtfulness. But that would get pretty old with everyone but me, so I temper myself and only refer to her infrequently. However, when the topic of wisdom popped up, I just couldn't pass her by.

Brother Harold was six years older than me. So, when he was twelve and in the seventh grade, I was six and in the first grade. On the occasion of that twelfth birthday, Mom and Dad got him a pen and pencil set. Anybody remember those? A pretty little box with three matching utensils inside—an ink pen, a ballpoint pen, and a mechanical pencil. Wow! He loved it, and I couldn't take my eyes off of it. I wanted one of those for myself, and I wanted it right *now*. But the lesson I learned, and the way I learned it, has stuck with me now for a lifetime. Mom, in her uniquely gentle way, took me aside, looked me directly in the eye, and said, "You are too young for a gift such as this. If you get everything you want *now*, you will never have anything to look forward to."

This was a perfect example of how my mother disciplined and taught. Never raised her voice. Never got physical. Just outsmarted me at every turn. I mean, what kind of answer could I possibly come back with? She was dead center on, and her honesty and her candor at confronting the situation left me with nothing to rebut. Even as brilliant as I thought I was at six years old, I knew she had topped me. I don't know where she got so smart, because it wasn't the last time in my life I would see her exert wisdom over a situation that lesser people would respond to with anger and too much action.

Teach us to number our days aright, that we may gain
a heart of wisdom.
—Psalm 90:12

So much is written in the Scriptures about wisdom. I would have to think one of the most popular stories on the subject comes from King Solomon. While he was in Gibeon offering up sacrifices, God came to him in a dream one night and said, "Ask for whatever you want me to give you."

Okay, let's hit pause and stop right there. If God came to any of us in a dream tonight with this kind of offer, what do you think you might say? It's a good introspective question to ask ourselves. Long life? Perfect health? Untold riches? Is there any chance it would be what we already know Solomon said? Because here is exactly what he said:

Give me a discerning heart to govern your people and to distinguish between right and wrong.
—1 Kings 3:9

God gave wisdom to Solomon plus all those good things he *didn't* ask for simply because he didn't ask for them. If we should ever make a list of all the things we would like to have in life, I'm not sure wisdom would be high on any of our lists. We'd probably say "better internet service" and "a cheaper health plan" way before we got around to listing wisdom. But those who innately have it as part of their natural makeup are something to behold. They are the ones we usually turn to when we want a good decision made. They're the ones we look to when we are electing church or club officers. They're the ones we consult as friends when we have a problem that needs solving. They're the ones who make good leaders. Good workers. And good mothers.

The Lord was pleased that Solomon had asked for this.
—1 Kings 3:10

Trickery

One of the strangest and most bizarre stories in the Old Testament can be found in the book of Judges. There is a lot of history leading up to the main event, but if we just review the essentials, it's still a most amazing and fascinating tale of OT warfare. It all has to do with a man named Jephthah (Jeff-tha).

Jephthah was born in the land of Gilead, and his father's *name* was Gilead. He had lots of half brothers, but what really made Jephthah stand out in the family was that his mother was a prostitute. When all of these boys grew into men, Jephthah's half brothers threw him out of the family and ran him out of the country so he wouldn't receive any of their father's inheritance. Jephthah settled in the land of Tob and became the leader of a gang of men who were known as feared warriors.

As will happen, when war broke out and the Ammonites attacked and Israel needed a strong commander on the battlefield, they went to Tob in search of the young man they had banished years before. God-fearing Jephthah accepted their offer and took Israel to victory.

The Ephraimites, one of the twelve tribes of Israel, declared war on Jephthah and his army because they thought

Jephthah had not asked them to fight that battle with him. And this is when the trickery began.

The Ephraimites tried to cross the Jordan River into Gilead territory, and in doing so tried to pass themselves off as soldiers of Jephthah. But before they could cross, they were asked to say a word that Jephthah's army knew they couldn't pronounce properly. Jephthah's soldiers would first stop them and say, "Are you an Ephraimite?" And if they said, "No," then they would say, "Say the word shibboleth." Invariably, the Ephraimite would say, "sibboleth" because the "sh" sound was not in their local dialect and their tongue just didn't bend that way. Because of this little trick, forty-two thousand Ephraimites were killed. Jephthah was not a man to be fooled with.

Debbie and I recently received one of the oldest telephone scams around. The phone rang, a local number showed up, and a live voice identified himself as a deputy with the county sheriff's department. He asked for Debbie, and as she and I both had picked up at the same time, she identified herself as being on the line. He proceeded to ask her if she had been called for jury duty in the past six months. She told him she had, and then he began to berate her for not showing up. She assured him the reason she had not shown up was because she had been notified that her assigned case had been settled and a jury was no longer needed. He bristled a little at this and then asked about her date of birth. I could immediately see this leading next toward her social security number and heaven knows what else, so at this point, I jumped in and asked him exactly who he was. He again stated he was with the sheriff's department in the county of Augusta and the city of STAWN-ton.

(For those of you who are not aware, our little hometown of Staunton, cradled in the heart of the Shenandoah Valley of Virginia, is not pronounced the way it's spelled; all the locals know very well it is called STAN-ton. Only the Ephraimites are unaware of this.)

Debbie and I both laughed, and I said, "I'm sorry, pal. You just blew your cover and gave yourself away with STAWN-ton." We hung up, and all I could think of was Meredith Willson's advice in *The Music Man* when the salesman on the train yelled at his fellow travelers, "But you've got to know the territory!" And you do. If you're going to scam someone, you had better know all the little local oddities and colloquial sayings and pronunciations or you will get caught with your shirttail hanging out and the law not far behind.

And then I remembered ole Jephthah and how the very same slip up had won him a battle. I had no battle to win as I went right back to reading my book with my dog on my lap after hanging up the phone. But Jephthah became a judge in Israel for his detection, and all because of an ear of corn. ("Ear of corn" is what the word shibboleth meant.)

May your week be in the Spirit and to him be the glory!

Valentine's Day

And it's Valentine's Day. Time to tell the one you love just how much you love them and try to count the ways. If you haven't been to the drugstore and bought a card, if you are not adept at making one on the computer, if you are lost for proper words of expression, then let me offer a solution you may have never tried. Go to about the center of your Bible and open it to something called Song of Songs. (Some translations have it titled Song of Solomon, although we are not sure he wrote any of this, but he might have.) Now begin to read, and you will find you have stumbled upon the most intimate and often erotic prose that you never thought was in the Holy Scriptures. It's quite open and graphic and suitable for a couple who want to express their sincere love for one another. (I say all of this tongue-in-cheek because I know you are probably well aware of this book in the Old Testament and what it says and how it says it. There are even those who have offered the interpretation that it is an allegory of the love between God and his people. Your call on that one.)

There are four different kinds of love described and explored in the Bible. Using the Greek identifications, they are:

1. Eros: sensual and romantic love between a couple
2. Philos: brotherly/friendly love between friends
3. Storge: familial love between family members
4. Agape: the most supreme of all, God's unconditional love for mankind

I think, should you read this book, written around 950 B.C., you'll agree it is man and woman stuff. The Jewish faith stresses that it represents not eros but agape telling, symbolically, of God's love for Israel. Some Christians, through the ages, have tried to tell us it represents the love between God and his church. Both concepts are a bit of a stretch for me. That's pretty hard to buy once you actually read the 117 verses, which you can do in less than fifteen minutes. And if you like what you read, you may want to borrow a verse or two if you decide to try your hand at making a homemade card for the man or woman of your dreams.

It begins, right out of the chute, with this line and then gets steamier as it goes:

Let him kiss me with the kisses of his mouth; for your love is more delightful than wine.
—Song of Songs 1:2

I have always been a movie fan from a very early age. In 1953, when I was only eight years old, there was a film I was aware of that was playing at a local theater. It was called *The Moon Is Blue* and starred William Holden and David Niven. I distinctly remember it was all over the news that it was being banned in many cities because it had an objectional word in it. The word was, believe it or not...virgin. Pretty mild by today's standards, isn't it?

It was then that I became curious about the meaning of the word and was rather disappointed when I discovered I had been hearing it in Sunday school, in sermons, and in every Christmas pageant I had ever attended or been a part of in my young life. How could such an important word in the Bible, essential to the most famous story in all history, shut down a movie theater? Life is strange. And I knew it even at eight years old.

So, the fact that the Song of Solomon is right smack dab in the middle of our Holy Bible should not be a problem to anyone. It's real life. It's to the point. It's a love story. And it gives the Scriptures even more scope, dimension, and meaning to our daily lives.

Queen of Sheba

King Solomon's name, wisdom, and relationship with God became known far and wide. The Queen of Sheba heard all about him and came to Jerusalem to visit him and test him with some hard questions she wanted answered. She arrived with a large caravan of camels, spices, gold, and all kinds of precious stones. The king sat with her and answered everything she asked, and the queen was taken by his famed wisdom. She was also overwhelmed by his palace, the food on his table, the robes on his servants, and the burnt offerings he made at the temple.

The queen even confided in Solomon that she had not believed all the amazing stories she had heard about him until she had come and seen all these things for herself. She told him his wisdom and wealth far exceeded anything she had ever heard about him and praised the Lord for putting such a man on the throne to rule Israel. They bestowed elaborate gifts on one another, and then the last sentence written in the Old Testament about the Queen of Sheba simply says:

Then she left and returned with her retinue to her own country.

—1 Kings 10:13

This is a very beautiful yet short story told in the books of 1 Kings 10 and in 2 Chronicles 9. The wording is virtually identical in both books. The fact that we don't know who wrote either of them is only one of several mysteries surrounding the story of these two royal figures. Tradition and legend kick in about here, and all kinds of fascinating notions and theories begin to fly about.

1. Where was the land of Sheba? Well, maybe in Yemen or Ethiopia. We frankly just don't know.

2. What was the queen's name? We are never told, which has made it impossible for traditional historians to trace her exact origin.

3. What were the hard questions the queen asked Solomon? There have been outside books that have speculated on their conversations, but the Bible never reveals that to us.

4. How long did the queen stay, and what was her relationship with Solomon? The length of her visit is never divulged, and some theologians seem to think the two became lovers and that it was she the king was writing about in the Song of Solomon. But again, this is not biblical and cannot be confirmed.

However, the Queen of Sheba finally gets respectful notice about a thousand years later when none other than Jesus, in Matthew 12 and Luke 11, refers to her as the queen of the South.

The queen of the South will rise up at the judgment with this generation and condemn it, for she came from the ends of the earth to hear the wisdom of Solomon, and behold, something greater than Solomon is here.
—Matthew 12:42

Jesus was giving her just dues because even though she had been a pagan and a Gentile, she had come to see Solomon and witness the goodness of his God while so many of Jesus' own people were unwilling to come and witness and receive what he had to offer.

As we said when we began this story, King Solomon's name, wisdom, and his relationship with God became known far and wide. Let's only hope our religion and beliefs precede us in all we do so that before we come and after we go, all who know us or hear of us will know our hearts are right with the Lord.

Hide it under a bushel, no!
I'm gonna let it shine
Let it shine, let it shine, let it shine
"This Little Light of Mine"
—Harry Dixon Loes

Gold Records

Many years ago, a business associate of ours (The Statlers) came to our office for a meeting. He brought along with him a nephew or cousin or some kin who was visiting his family from out of town. The young man, about twenty years of age, roamed around out in the halls and waited until our meeting was finished. We came out, shook hands, and said our farewells, and they both left. That night, our offices were broken into and some gold records were stolen off our walls. We and the police had every reason to believe it was this young man, who mysteriously left town before sunrise that very day.

The assessment from the police was that someone, in the middle of the night, forcefully kicked in the backdoor, which immediately set off the alarm system. The fact that apparently the burglar ran down the hall and snatched an armful of gold records off the wall and ran out the way he came in before the police could arrive was very telling. They were sure he had cased the place and knew just how long it would take him to make his dash in, grab the goods, and dash out. It cost us (or should I say the insurance company) the price of a new backdoor and that was all. The surprise, or joke, was on him, because when he saw his booty in the morning daylight and broke open the frames of the gold albums, he had a rude and rather humorous awakening on his hands.

Here's the secret: those gold albums are not all they seem. They are just plain ole record albums like you have on your den shelves from days gone by, basically spray painted with gold paint. The value is not in the record itself but in the honor placed on them. They are given to celebrate sales. And when those sales doubled, they gave us platinum albums, which are just like the others but sprayed with *silver* paint.

Breaking down the cost, I would estimate—considering how record companies order plain vinyl records in bulk and how inexpensive it would be to apply metallic paint—that each "gold" record he stole cost all of around fifty cents. I'm sure the frame was the most expensive item in the whole package, and if they ordered those in bulk too, could the overall worth really be more than five dollars per?

After the shavings were swept up from the new door, we contacted our record company, Mercury, and they replaced the gold albums within two weeks and life was back up and running.

What is that wonderful old saying about "all that glitters is not gold"? Many will tell you it's in the Bible, but don't waste your time looking for it. It's actually Shakespeare, from *The Merchant of Venice*. But it's still very true and certainly good advice.

The police never caught the apparent "thief in the night," and we didn't press it any further, to save embarrassment to our business associate. But remembering back on it, I find it easy today to see the lesson from it all. We should never make assumptions and follow through on them. That poor guy assumed he was going to be rich with stacks of gold in the trunk of his car, but he wound up with maybe twenty dollars' worth of nothing. Jesus tells us in John 7:24, "Judge not according to appearance."

This holds true if we're looking at things that glitter and catch our attention, or if we're looking at people who leave that first, shallow impression. How many times have we, ourselves, walked away from a situation and hoped that our actions or words wouldn't be remembered and that we wouldn't be judged by what we had just said or acted out? We owe it to ourselves and all those around us not to judge quickly and without fairness and sensitivity. Give someone a chance or two. And think twice about whatever that pretty item is that might tempt you into acting too hastily.

The words and wisdom of King Solomon should be a guide to us all.

> *My son, do not lose sight of these—keep sound wisdom and discretion, and they will be life for your soul and adornment for your neck. Then you will walk on your way securely, and your foot will not stumble. When you lie down, you will not be afraid; when you lie down, your sleep will be sweet.*
>
> —Proverbs 3:21–24

A good dose of wisdom and discretion will give us a good night's sleep. As simple as that sounds, sometimes that is just everything!

Thanks be to God!

Outside Church

From the first Sunday in June to the last Sunday in October 2020, our church was blessed to be able to meet outside almost every Sunday morning for worship services. That big grassy field by the picnic shelter that used to be a ball diamond when I was growing up was just tailor-made for what we used it for during that crazy and difficult pandemic time. Everyone brought their lawn chairs and kept their distance. There were umbrellas scattered about to ward off the sun and an occasional raindrop. And everyone's faces showed how glad they were to just be there. I can sincerely say it was fun! I know it was for me, and I think I would have been ecstatic had we ever done this when I was a kid. To sit outside on the old ballfield in the sunshine and be able to actually come to church in shorts and a ballcap would have made me happy way down inside. And here I am, a big old kid, and it made me just as pleased in my heart as if I were a little kid again myself.

I sat there on Sunday mornings in my fold-up canvas chair and looked across that beautiful green field and thought that this is just how Jesus did it. He would sit down or maybe he would stand or maybe he leaned on a large rock and just talk to all who gathered. And boy, did they gather. Sometimes four thousand. Sometimes five thousand. And only God himself knows how many may have heard the Sermon on the Mount firsthand and in person. And I came away each morning from those alfresco worship services a little more touched and inspired than usual. Maybe it was the different setting from what we have become accustomed to. Or maybe it was the freshness of the real air. Or the distant sounds of traffic. Or birds flying overhead. All those things came together and made us more aware of him and made us more sensitive to the message we wound up leaving with. The setting had an effect on me as much as the stories themselves. I could actually see those thousands sitting quietly in the open air and listening to every word and feeding on every thought as Jesus' voice echoed through the crowd. Time was lost on them, as Matthew 14:15 tells us:

> *As evening approached, the disciples came to him and said, "This is a remote place, and it's already getting late. Send the crowds away, so they can go to the villages and buy themselves some food."*

But Jesus fed the multitude. We all know the story. Each Sunday morning, the elders on duty at our church count those in attendance to keep for the church records. And the Scriptures tell us the count that day was five thousand men. They didn't even count the women and children. The same goes just one chapter later, when Matthew tells a similar story of a gathering of four thousand. Jesus climbs a hillside and this time sits down for sure and preaches and heals, and this service goes on for three days. Quit looking at your watch every ten minutes. It lasted for *three days*, as Matthew 15:32 says:

*Jesus called his disciples to him and said, "I have com-
passion for these people; they have already been with me
three days and have nothing to eat. I do not want to
send them away hungry, or they may collapse on the
way."*

And as we know, Jesus sends no one away hungry. He
fed them all and had basketfuls left over. And again, the
amazing count of four thousand in attendance didn't even
include the women and children. I close my eyes sometimes
and think just how slim our crowds would be in churches
today if we didn't count the women. The women who teach
and hold offices and do the work and the organizing and
who are so often the only adult accounted for when a family
walks down the aisle to the pews.

I enjoyed those outdoor services that allowed us to meet
without all the restrictions we would have had to endure during those times if we had gone inside. I don't know what the
future months or even years hold for us, but we can only be
thankful and feel blessed for the time we have spent under
the blue skies, doing it the way Jesus did it.

*For the beauty of the earth,
For the beauty of the skies,
For the love which from our birth
Over and around us lies,
Lord of all, to thee we raise
This our hymn of grateful praise.*
"For the Beauty of the Earth"
—Folliott Pierpoint

Patriotism versus Politics

It was a family-fun kind of thing. We laughed about it at the time and for years to come. The 1964 presidential election was upon us, and it was the talk that filled not just the newspapers and television, but our house as well. Republican Barry Goldwater was challenging incumbent Democrat Lyndon Johnson. My brother and sister were each married, but I was still at home and the discussions about the pros and cons of the candidates were lively. It was suspected early on that Mom and Dad might be voting different tickets this time around. We couldn't be sure, but it was all our suspicions that Mom was going for Johnson and Dad for Goldwater. My brother, never one to let anything lay quietly, tried teasing and cajoling our mother into admitting her preference out loud. All this was to no avail as she would only offer an evasive comment and a smile. No amount of wheedling and sweet-talk from her oldest son would move her. The election came and went, and to this day none of us are any wiser as to how Mom cast her vote. For decades after, Harold would ask her, out of the clear blue, "Mom, who was it now that you voted for in '64?" And she would slyly answer, "If I wanted you to know, I would have told you twenty years ago."

This kind of amusement over politics and candidates is a thing of the past. Today, with the nastiness and insulting nature of both parties toward the other, it is a home-splitting issue. Then add the strength and indecent power of social media, and friendly disagreements turn quickly into anger and even violence. What has happened? When did it happen? Why did it happen? And how long, in the name of all that is sensible, will it last? I can honestly say my wife and I are usually on the same political page, however, there are times when we aren't. She has her views, I have mine. We still eat together. Still sleep in the same bed. Still live peacefully and lovingly in the same house, just like my parents. But I see it separating loved ones today. Friendships are shattered, old pals of years gone by no longer speak to one another, and what party you're going to vote for has become the most important aspect of people's lives. It defines who they are. What up, folks? What up?

The entire forty-year career of The Statler Brothers was one spent waving the flag and professing our patriotism. We opened every concert with the National Anthem and had a huge star-spangled banner as our backdrop. Yet we never once spoke of a favored party or offered public allegiance and endorsement to any candidate. We were summoned to the White House on numerous occasions to perform and have dinner. Sometimes just for meetings and luncheons. I say this in all humbleness to make the point that never once did we consider the party in power at the time. We didn't even consider the person in power at the time. It was the office we were honoring. For all those who have forgotten, that is called patriotism.

Politics, on the other hand, has become the questionable art of shunning those, and calling them names, who don't believe in every policy tactic that arises each day. Politics is believing you can't put cows and horses in the same field and expect them to get along. You can. Which only proves animals are more conducive to common sense than calculated politicians. Because the only places I'm aware of that have a center aisle separating their occupants are the Senate and the House of Representatives. We Americans don't separate gender in public. Don't separate races in public. Don't separate religion in public. Don't separate attitudes or classes in public. Only in Congress. And that is called Politics with a capital P.

The day has passed where everyone understands that patriotism and politics are two different words. If you're caught waving the flag or being nice to someone of another persuasion, you are cancelled, ridiculed, and destroyed. You must show wrath and annoyance to everyone who doesn't agree with you 100 percent of the time on 100 percent of the issues. This kind of thinking is tiresome and small-minded and keeps us all looking back to some good old days of yore.

Remember Ronald Reagan and Tip O'Neill? They could argue their points all morning long and then play golf together that afternoon. There are many pictures of them with their arms around one another. They liked and respected each other and the times allowed them to show it. Can you even imagine such a thing happening in Washington today?

The time has come to turn back to God and reassert our trust in him for the healing of America.
—Ronald Reagan

The Rock

"Peter, the rock." This phrase brings a lot of translational interpretation to the table. It is commonly known that the Roman Catholic Church believes Peter was the rock and very foundation of their church, that he was the first pope. So, just where do we as Protestants stand on the matter? To ascertain that, we have to look closely at the Scripture that has been in contention for centuries by theologians and scholars alike:

> "But what about you?" he asked. "Who do you say I am?" Simon Peter answered, "You are the Christ, the Son of the living God." Jesus replied, "Blessed are you, Simon son of Jonah, for this was not revealed to you by man, but by my Father in heaven. And I tell you that you are Peter, and on this rock I will build my church, and the gates of Hades will not overcome it. I will give you the keys of the kingdom of heaven; whatever you bind on earth will be bound in heaven, and whatever you loose on earth will be loosed in heaven." Then he ordered his disciples not to tell anyone that he was the Christ.
>
> —Matthew 16:15–20

Yes, God used Peter strongly in the founding of the church. He was the first to proclaim the Gospel on the day of Pentecost. He was the first to take the Word to the Gentiles. God used him effectively, as he did the other apostles, including Paul. So, consider the Protestant belief that when Jesus spoke of building his church on a rock, that rock was the confession of faith that Peter had just declared and not the man himself. "You are the Christ, the Son of the living God." That belief and that faith is the foundation of the church.

> *For no one can lay any foundation other than the one already laid, which is Jesus Christ.*
> —1Corinthians 3:11

Peter is given credit for unlocking the doors of salvation to three different worlds: the Jews, the Samaritans, and the Gentiles. He shares a great revelation with us in the book of Acts when he says:

> *I now realize how true it is that God does not show favoritism but accepts men from every nation who fear him and do what is right.*
> —Acts 10:34–35

Here is one of my favorite Peter stories from Acts. He and John went to Samaria and laid hands on people, and the Holy Spirit took over and completed the job. Watching all this from the sidelines was a local magician, Simon the Sorcerer. He had an act that was admired in the area, and he thought if he could learn Peter's and John's "trick," it would really add to his popularity. He pulled Peter aside and basically asked him how much it would cost for them to show him how they did that trick. To say that Peter took this inquiry badly would be an understatement. Peter lashed out at the magician and said, "May your money perish with you because you thought you could buy the gift of God with money! You have no part in this ministry because your heart is not right with God. Pray and perhaps God will forgive you for having such a thought." Needless to say, Simon the Sorcerer was crushed and begged Peter to pray on his behalf.

I have a very distinct picture of Peter in my mind and have had for years. I see him as tall and thick in size with hard muscles and shoulders that could withstand the weight of three normal men. I can almost see the features of his face, sun-beaten and wind-burned, with eyes that could pierce a hole in you. He would have been a physical force for any man to come up against. (How does this compare to your image of him?) He didn't shy away from difficult situations. He wasn't afraid. He faced adversity head-on, ready to fight and take on any man who stood in the way of God's cause and his mission. But wait. Maybe I've over-spoken a bit because this same Peter did have a few weak moments that we know all too well about. There was a time or three when he failed to stand up and speak the truth, although we can only think hard of him for this if we have never taken a false step ourselves. But more about that later.

QUESTION FOR THOUGHT

Peter is known in the Scriptures by five names. What are they?

ANSWER

Simon, Peter, Simon Peter, Cephas, and Simeon.

The Left-Handed Judge

Another Old Testament story begins, *And the children of Israel did evil again in the sight of the Lord.* This time it's in the book of Judges, chapter 3. And this time it's a classic tale of a wicked king who had reigned for eighteen years over a bemoaning Jewish nation until God finally decided to deliver them yet again in a most unusual way.

King Eglon was the villainous ruler whom Scriptures describe as "a very fat man." Ehud was the judge, chosen by God, to carry out the duties of assassin, and his particular trait, described in the Scriptures, was being "lefthanded." We must remember all this because both of these descriptions are important to the story.

Ehud, on a mission from God, cooked up a fake tribute for the king and sent word to the palace he wanted to personally bring it to the throne. We don't know exactly what this tribute was. It might have been a bag of money, a statue, a poem—we're never told. But before Ehud and his staff entered the gates, he took an eighteen-inch, razor-sharp, double-edged knife and strapped it to the inside of his right thigh. Being lefthanded, this made it easy for him to grasp it with one easy move. Also, apparently, the rarity of being lefthanded gave him the needed cover for reaching inside his clothes in the presence of the king. A quick move with the right hand might have gotten him arrested, but not with the left. After presenting the king with the tribute and seeing how happy and smiling he was, Ehud dismissed the men who had come with him and then turned to King Eglon and said quietly, "O king, I have a secret to tell you." The king, eager to hear more praise of himself, dismissed all of his staff, which left just the two of them in the room. Ehud waited till all had left and all the doors were closed and then got up and walked over to Eglon and said, "I have a message for you from God."

He then reached his left hand into his clothing, took the weapon by the handle, drew it, and ran the blade into the royal belly. Eighteen inches of blade and handle so deep it couldn't be pulled out of his enormous stomach. Air whooshed from the king and he never made another sound. Ehud made sure he was dead before calmly walking out of the room, locking the doors behind him, and confidently strolling out of the palace and off the grounds. The king's servants, after finding the doors to his room locked, assumed he was unavailable in the bathroom and waited patiently outside. After a long while, they went for a key and entering, found him dead.

All of this sounds like a classic scene from *The Godfather*, but I promise it's from the Holy Scriptures.

But back to Ehud, our hero. He went to the mountain, blew the trumpet, and all the men of Israel joined him as he led the army of God against Eglon's army, killing ten thousand. And Ehud reigned peacefully for the next eighty years. What a story!

The summers I was ten and eleven years old, we had a youth minister at Olivet. His name was Henry Brockmann, and he was from High Point, North Carolina. He was a seminary student who spent those couple of summers working at the church teaching Bible school, coaching our junior softball team, teaching Sunday school, and just being an all-around good advisor to all the youth. We loved him, and I have often felt remiss for not looking him up and staying in touch in my adult years. I remember so much of all he taught us, and one thing I clearly recall him saying was, "There is every kind of story you will ever want to read right there in the Bible. Adventure. Mystery. Murder. Deceit. Good guys versus bad guys. It's all right here!"

I was reading the Hardy Boys series at that time in my life, but I understood what Henry was saying. And maybe because of him I have always been fascinated with those little-told Old Testament stories that really are as good as any adventure tale you'll ever find in any other book. Thank you, Henry. I hope life was good to you, and I really am sorry we didn't stay in touch.

God teaches in so many ways.

Besetting Sin

First, let's define the title so we'll all be on the same page. There is sin, and then there is besetting sin. The dictionary tells us a besetting sin means "a main or constant problem or fault." That's simple enough to grasp. Ask yourself what constant fault or sin you most struggle with, and then you have a good idea of what besetting sin is all about. The interesting thing is that we all will come up with a different answer, because it will be a personal and individual sin that we may not even want to talk about with other people.

I often think just how much I miss the discussions we all enjoy so much sitting around the Sunday school room on Sunday mornings, but maybe the absence of those discussions is a blessing this time. This pandemic-imposed privacy may give us all a more reflective moment to look at ourselves in a more honest and open way. There's an old joke that goes with this topic just perfectly: Four preachers walk into a bar...no, a tavern...no, a restaurant. Sitting around a table, one suggests they all share their besetting sin. The first one says, "Well, sometimes I slip out of my office in the middle of the day and go to the racetrack and drop a few bucks on my favorite horse."

The second preacher says, "My besetting sin is I keep a bottle of wine hidden in the basement. When I get fed up with my deacons and elders, I sometimes slip down there and take a little nip."

The third says, "I guess mine is that I keep a punching bag at home, and when I have had enough of a particularly annoying church member, I go home, think about that person, and punch that bag for all it's worth."

The fourth minister remained obviously quiet. The other three had to press him for his answer, and he finally said, "Okay, my besetting sin is gossip and I can't wait to tell everybody about this conversation!"

> *It is better to trust in the Lord than to put confidence in man.*
>
> —Psalm 118:8

Besetting sin is that symbolic low-hanging pipe in the basement you keep bumping your head on. That lingering something that just won't get out of your way and you have to constantly keep dodging it. Maybe it really is gossiping or lying or lust or losing your temper. Take the seven deadly sins, which, incidentally, are not biblical, so don't try to look them up. But it may be one of those, and here is that list, as you may already know, for the record:

PRIDE/ENVY/GLUTTONY/LUST/
ANGER/GREED/SLOTH

Is the idea of the seven deadly sins biblically based? Yes and no. Proverbs 6:16–19 lists seven things that are detestable to God: 1) haughty eyes, 2) a lying tongue, 3) hands that shed innocent blood, 4) a heart that plots evil, 5) feet that are quick to rush to do wrong, 6) a false witness, and 7) a man who stirs up dissension among brothers. Of course, none of these are deadly. They all are just as forgivable as any other sin we might come up with. There is only one unforgivable and unpardonable sin, but we'll save that topic for another time.

And we certainly won't ask one another, "What's your besetting sin?" the way those four ministers did. But today would be the perfect opportunity to ask ourselves that very personal and pertinent question. And if we want to change, I firmly believe that all change comes from within. I also believe human beings never really change without the divine intervention of the Holy Spirit. Have you ever known someone who was not a believer who changed their ways for the better? Who softened their own hearts? Who adopted more loving thoughts on their own? I haven't and don't expect to.

Sin is a human part of our lives. First John 1:8 affirms, that *if we claim to be without sin, we deceive ourselves and the truth is not in us.* But if we confess that one that keeps hanging on and gnawing at us, we will be given the strength to shake even it.

Thanks be to God. To him be the glory.

Thanksgiving Day

Every Thanksgiving my mind immediately goes back to the children of Israel and their plight through the wilderness. They were slaves in Egypt for 430 years. Four hundred and thirty years! More than four centuries! Then God hand-picked Moses to go in there and lead them out. Of course, Moses fumbled around and moaned a little bit and tried to get out of it, but God was having none of that. So, Moses suited up and went in; went through all the plagues—the frogs, flies, gnats, boils, and more. God explained the bloody Passover to him, then parted the Red Sea for his escape, and finally, they were free after 430 years. *To the very day* (Gen. 12:40–41). Free from the horrible chains of Egypt and ready for a period of Thanksgiving.

But, wait! Not really.

After a month and a half, they were grumbling and complaining. Granted, life was not easy on the run out there in the wilderness, but after only six weeks, they were saying, "We sure do wish we were back in Egypt. There we had pots of meat to eat." Life was just too rough and the price of freedom was just too high.

Now, jump ahead many, many centuries to what we call the Pilgrims, who were also on the run for their religious freedom. They crossed the Atlantic Ocean in crude, small, and cramped ships. And they didn't do it in a ten-day cruise. It took a long, long time. There was no heat, no protection from the sun, and only the wind to steer them. And God didn't part any rough waters and let them walk through. When they landed, they started from scratch. They cut down trees to build cabins, planted food to keep from starving, shot deer and bear for food and clothing. After a year of this kind of living, they decided things weren't all that bad and they were pretty darned glad to be here. So, they declared a day to thank God for all he had given them.

After six weeks, Israel was ready to throw in the towel. After a year, the Pilgrims were ready to praise God. Israel built a golden idol out there in the wilds to worship. The Pilgrims built churches so they could go inside and worship the Lord. I make these comparisons not to disparage the Jewish nation in any way, but to shed proper light on the bravery and the character of these religious freedom seekers we call the Pilgrims. They were one tough bunch of folks. Not the prissy little men in knee-high pants and funny hats comedians like to do jokes about around this time of year. They were strong and resilient, and they made their proud place in our American history. Without them we just may never have been a God-fearing nation. And without more like them, cut from the same pattern of strength and faith, we may not *remain* a God-fearing nation, if we're not careful.

Never does a Thanksgiving come or go that I don't ask myself this question, and today I'll ask you: if we didn't already have a Thanksgiving Day established here in America, what do you think the chances would be of getting one established today? Would Congress, both our House and Senate, pass a declaration to have a day of worship and of giving thanks to God? Could we find enough elected leaders to vigorously push the matter in the face of the adversity and indifference that it would surely meet? The answer in my mind is that there is not a snowball's chance in Miami that would ever happen.

So, thank the good and fearless Pilgrims, their wives and children, for what they faced and endured to give us what we take for granted. And thanks be to God for the grace and goodness he gives us every day of our lives.

> *Enter into his gates with thanksgiving and into his*
> *courts with praise.*
> *Be thankful unto Him and bless His name*
> *For the Lord is good; His mercy is everlasting*
> *And His truth endureth to all generations.*
> —Psalm 100: 4–5

A Happy and Wonderful Thanksgiving Day to you and to everyone you love!

Sunday Morning Service

Steve Allen, as some of you will remember, was a comedian, the first *Tonight Show* host, a pianist, songwriter, author, actor, and all-around consummate entertainer. The Statlers did a TV show with him in 1980 and just fell in love with him. There was a legend floating around the business that he always carried a small tape recorder in his pocket so he could record comedy and song ideas any time of the day or night. One day we were all talking with him, and brother Harold said, "You are the best all-around entertainer of our lifetime." Steve immediately pulled out that little recorder, held it up, and said, "Would you repeat that, please?" The legend was true.

Another legend about him was that early in his career he bet singer Frankie Laine one thousand dollars that he could sit in the window of Wallich's Music City record store at the corner of Sunset and Vine with a piano and write fifty songs a day for an entire week. Frankie took him up on it and lost a thousand dollars. At least one of those 350 songs he wrote that week became a top-twenty hit on the pop charts for the duet of Margaret Whiting and Jimmy Wakely. (You've probably never heard of either of them, but it was a big song back in 1950.) The title was "Let's Go to Church Next Sunday Morning." It was actually a love song set against the scene of going to church together, a theme and title that would never get recorded in today's music industry. And it just goes to show that God is in everything we do and in every place we are, even in the window of Wallich's music store.

> Let's go to church next Sunday morning, let's kneel and
>   pray side by side
> Our love will grow on Sunday morning, if we have the
>   Lord as our guide
> Through the week we love and laugh and labor
> But on Sunday don't forget to love thy neighbor
> Let's make a date for Sunday morning, and we'll go to
>   church, you and I

"If we have the Lord as our guide" is the key line to this song for me, because I have found that if we walk into church on a Sunday morning with a bad attitude toward something or someone and come out with that same attitude, then a number of things have *not* happened.

We have *not* listened to the sermon.
We have *not* listened to the prayers.
We have *not* listened to the words of the hymns.

But here's a number of things that *have* happened:

We *have* just put in time being there.
We *have* let our minds wander.
We *have* closed our hearts to everything around us.

If we ever come away from a worship service and can't remember one good thing about the sermon or what was prayed for or what we sang, then we should look to ourselves for the answer. It is likely our own fault, because it is nearly impossible to not glean something helpful from an hour of worship and praise. In many services you will see in the bulletin a Prayer of Preparation. Listen closely to these words, as it may be the most important prayer of the morning. It is always a plea to God to prepare us for worship. To cleanse our minds of all the things that are crowding it and making life miserable for us. To open up our hearts and get us ready to receive. To bring us together as one with God's spirit and give us some peace and a deep breath. If we can do this, it is a given that something good will happen in the next hour that will put a comfort to whatever is troubling us.

> *Let's go to church next Sunday morning, we'll see our*
> *   friends on the way*
> *We'll stand and sing on Sunday morning, and I'll hold*
> *   your hand while we pray*
> *Through the years we'll always be together*
> *You'll be mine and we won't fear the stormy weather*
> *Let's go to church next Sunday morning, let's go through*
> *   life side by side*

Lent

The church I grew up in, which is the church I'm still in today, never stressed Lent. I always thought it was the Catholics, the Episcopalians, and the Lutherans who were more likely to observe the Lenten season than we Presbyterians. I can never remember as a kid being asked what I was going to sacrifice for Lent. I can never remember special services during the spring that emphasized this period that got everyone ready for Easter. As a matter of fact, even though I knew a little of what it was about, I can remember the very first time I gave any thought whatsoever to it, and by that time I was a teenager.

We were in high school, and I was driving home one afternoon with a carload of friends, boys and girls together. I stopped on the way at a little mart to get a drink, and as I got out of the car, I asked if anybody wanted anything. A couple of them said, "Bring me a Coke." As I got almost to the door of the little market, one of the girls stuck her head out the car window and yelled, "No, no, no. Don't bring me a Coke. I gave them up for Lent. Bring me a Pepsi."

I remember thinking at the time, "Is *that* the way it works? Certainly not."

Many, many years later, as I began to teach a Sunday school class at same, said church, I started an acknowledgement of Lent that went on for years. Our class members, always adventurous and game, would agree to give something up or take something on as a lifestyle change for forty days. We would make a list and then review them for the next six Sundays to see who could make it and who might fall by the wayside. It was our way of supporting one another and, to be honest, it was interesting and a true study in commitment and perseverance. Every week, somebody would say, "Take me off the list. I caved this week and ate a whole box of candy." Or, "I went as long as I could but I just had to have a cup of coffee yesterday morning." No one was shamed, because we all knew we might be the one next Sunday to holler "uncle." But to the positive side, there were always those who made it all the way.

In the beginning, we went the entire six and a half weeks. Then, after a few years, we did the more sensible version of taking Sundays off and being able to give it a rest without the feelings of guilt and failure.

Some of the favorite items we abstained from during Lent from those years past were soft drinks, sweets, salt, red meat, junk food, and all carbs. Some memorable ones were those who gave up soap operas, bread, and all fast food. And then some people took on certain things such as daily exercise, daily devotions, and memorizing a new Bible verse every day. That last one was my wife, Debbie, and she still does new verses every Lent.

But my favorite of all was the person who gave up chocolate one year. Then he found a bakery that served donuts with carob powder on them and claimed it was not cheating because even though the taste was the same, it really wasn't chocolate. Oh, yeah, I remember now. That was me!

In all seriousness, the observance of Lent is a reverent, humble, and solemn time for spiritual discipline. It readies us for the most holy of our days, Good Friday and the Resurrection. Should you decide to take part, I offer my prayers for the success and fulfillment it brings to your Easter season. Lent begins on Ash Wednesday and continues to Easter morning. Ashes for repentance and sacrifice are mentioned numerous times in the Bible.

So I turned to the Lord God and pleaded with him in prayer and petition, in fasting and in sackcloth and ashes.

—Daniel 9:3

Blessings and may God be in your every endeavor.

Thursday Night and Friday Morning

Palm Sunday, and the crowds were waiting for Jesus to enter the city. They praised him and welcomed him with the glory he deserved, although they were misled in their hearts as to whom and why they were offering such praise. Peter and the other disciples were present but did not understand at all what it meant. They had no way of knowing what this most dramatic week would hold forth and how lives forever in the future of time would be changed through the events they would personally witness. They would see the crowd turn and this hero-of-the-moment be arrested, tortured, and nailed to a cross of execution. And Peter would be deeply involved in every aspect of each twist and turn of the next miraculous seven days.

It was after the last supper they had together on Thursday night. Peter was again handpicked by Jesus to go with him, this time into the Garden of Gethsemane to stay on watch while Jesus prayed. But Peter, James, and John fell asleep on the job and Jesus had to wake them. Jesus said, "Couldn't you stay awake for just one hour?"

After leaving again, Jesus went away to pray and when he came back, he found them asleep again. And a third time he came back and found all three of them asleep. "Get up! Let's go!" he said to them. "The hour has come."

They were out at the Mount of Olives, when a large group, including the chief priests and officers of the army, accosted them. The soldiers were armed with swords and clubs, carrying lanterns and torches, when out of the dark stepped Judas, who approached Jesus and kissed him on the cheek to identify him to his enemies. This was all it took for Peter to fly into action as he quickly pulled a sword and cut off the right ear of the servant of the high priest. Jesus again had to deal with Peter's temper, and he reprimanded him on the spot.

"Put your sword away," he said to him. "Don't you think I could call on my Father and he would send twelve legions of angels to protect me if I wanted to? But then how would the Scriptures be fulfilled that say it must happen this way?"

With these words, Jesus reached out, touched the man's ear, and healed him.

Can we even imagine how Peter felt, knowing how he had so severely disappointed the Son of God? Well, yes, I imagine we can, can't we? We all have felt that hot flash of humiliation when we know in our heart of hearts that we have just disappointed Jesus.

> *"You will all fall away," Jesus told them, "for it is written:*
> *'I will strike the shepherd, and the sheep will be scattered.'*
> *But after I have risen, I will go ahead of you into Galilee."*
> *Peter declared, "Even if all fall away, I will not."*
> *"Truly I tell you," Jesus answered, "today—yes, tonight—*
> *before the rooster crows twice, you yourself, will disown me*
> *three times."*
> *But Peter insisted emphatically, "Even if I have to die with*
> *you, I will never disown you." And all the others said the*
> *same.*
>
> —Mark 14:27–31

And Peter meant it with all his heart and soul. He meant it as he was sitting in the courtyard warming himself by the fire, waiting as Jesus was questioned by the Sanhedrin. He meant it all the way up to when a servant girl recognized him and said, "You were with Jesus of Galilee."

"I don't know what you're talking about," Peter snapped back at her.

He walked away only to have another girl approach him and say, "You were with Jesus of Nazareth."

"I don't know the man, I tell you," Peter said with a force that surprised even him.

Others started coming up to him saying, "You're one of them, aren't you? Your accent gives you away."

At this, he began to curse and swore to them, "I do not know the man."

Then somewhere in the distance a rooster crowed and Peter remembered the words of Jesus and went outside and wept bitterly.

All in one night, Peter had let Jesus down by falling asleep, by drawing a weapon on an adversary and cutting off a man's ear, and by cursing and breaking a promise to him by denying him three times. All in one night! Maybe we can't say we have done the same (I certainly hope not), but we have felt the pain of failure and the shame of letting our Savior down. We all know what it feels like to carry the guilt of a harsh word spoken too quickly or an action we wish we could take back and do over. And it is little comfort sometimes to tell ourselves he loves us and knows how weak and helpless we are, but in all truthfulness, that is simply the case. He loved and then forgave Peter, not because of his strengths but because of his weaknesses. Not because of who he was but because of who he could become. And he does the same for us every day, every hour.

QUESTION FOR THOUGHT

What was the name of the man whose ear was sliced off by Peter?

ANSWER

Malchus

Mother's Day

I hope we'll all take some special moments today to remember and pay respects to our own mothers. But as we do, I thought it might be interesting to renew some facts about why we even have this wonderful day saluting all the mothers who gave us life and, in most cases, gave us life lessons we will use and cherish till the very end.

It was Anna Jarvis who started it all. Anna was from Grafton, West Virginia, just 135 miles across a couple of mountains from where I live here in Virginia. And on an even more local note, Anna attended college at what is now Mary Baldwin University, located in downtown Staunton. Anna's mother, Anna Reeves Jarvis, was a big activist during the Civil War. She cared for soldiers on both sides, and living in West Virginia made both sides rather accessible to her. Anna had carried the idea of honoring this inspiring woman's life in some fashion, and when her mother passed away in 1905, it didn't take her long to act on the plan she had in the back of her mind.

Anna began a letter-writing campaign and went on a promotional tour across the United States. She met with moneyed people such as John Wanamaker, the department store chain owner of Wanamaker's (which eventually became Macy's), and H. J. Heinz, the ketchup king, to begin her financial backing. Her dream was for a national Mother's Day that would have its roots in churches and encourage everyone to visit or write their mother on this special day. To better understand the intentions of Anna Jarvis, here is a direct quote: "A maudlin, insincere printed card or a ready-made telegram means nothing except that you're too lazy to write to the woman who has done more for you than anyone else in the world. Any mother would rather have a line of the worst scribble from her son or daughter than any fancy greeting card."

By 1908, her plan was for Mother's Day to be celebrated the second Sunday in May. By 1914 she had lobbied Woodrow Wilson to proclaim it a national holiday. In her time, Anna angrily took on the greeting card industry and the floral industry for commercializing her sacred day. She even attacked Eleanor Roosevelt for using Mother's Day to raise money for a favorite charity of the first lady's. And she was once dragged kicking and screaming out of a meeting of the American War Mothers and arrested for disturbing the peace. It seems they were selling carnations to raise money on Mother's Day, and Anna wanted no part of that for her venerable day.

In 1923, Anna sued the state of New York for having a Mother's Day celebration. In 1930, the United States Post Office issued a Mother's Day stamp with a picture of Whistler's Mother. Anna Jarvis hounded the USPO until they finally removed the words "Mother's Day" from the stamp. And once, while dining at the Tea Room at Wanamaker's in Philadelphia, she saw a "Mother's Day Salad" on the menu. She ordered it, and when it was served, she stood up and dumped it on the floor and walked out.

Because of her obsession of total control, Anna had lost *all* control of the commemoration she had created to honor her mother. She said many times, "I wanted it to be a day of sentiment; not profit." In her final days, she walked door to door in the streets of Philadelphia gathering signatures trying to rescind and abolish Mother's Day. In the end, sadly, Anna died in West Chester, Pennsylvania, on November 24, 1948, institutionalized and deeply in debt. Ironically, her bill at the home was paid by the National Florist Exchange, the very industry she had railed so against.

But we must remember and appreciate Anna Jarvis's heart and good intentions. Her story is sad, but thanks to her efforts, each year we take a Sunday in May to honor our own loving mothers, and in doing so, we are reminded of so many beautiful verses from the Holy Scriptures.

> *Strength and dignity are her clothing, and she laughs at the time to come. She opens her mouth with wisdom, and the teaching of kindness is on her tongue. She looks well to the ways of her household and does not eat the bread of idleness. Her children rise up and call her blessed; her husband also, and he praises her: "Many women have done excellently, but you surpass them all."*
> —Proverbs 31:25–30

> *My son, keep your father's commandment, and forsake not your mother's teaching.*
> —Proverbs 6:20

> *When Jesus saw his mother and the disciple whom he loved standing nearby, he said to his mother, "Woman, behold, your son!" Then he said to the disciple, "Behold,*

*your mother!" And from that hour the disciple took her
to his own home.*

—John 19:26–27

This last passage is among my favorite of all time. It tells us that one of Jesus' final thoughts while hanging and dying on the cross was of his mother. The mother who had carried and pondered so much in her heart all of his life. Even Jesus felt a closeness to his mother and a need to connect with her near his final breath.

May God richly bless our mothers and their loving and caring hearts today and all the days of their lives and all the days their memories lay so sweetly on our hearts.

Fun Mystery Questions of the Bible

Wherever the Bible is studied and discussed, questions will invariably be raised no matter the age or denomination of the group. Here are just a few of what I call fun mystery topics that never lose their flavor and fascination.

1. Whom did Cain marry?

The Bible says after Cain killed his brother Abel, he *"went out from the Lord's presence and lived in the land of Nod, east of Eden. Cain lay with his wife and she became pregnant and gave birth to Enoch"* (Gen. 4:16–17).

Speculation: The only possible answer here is probably a sister, a niece, or even a great- niece. This sounds pretty crude by today's way of thinking, but in all honesty, it wasn't until the eighteenth chapter of Leviticus, when God handed down the laws to Moses, that concerns about interfamily marrying and sexual practices were addressed. And this was easily six hundred years after Cain's incident.

Answer: We have no idea.

2. What was Moses' speech problem?

The Bible says when God chose Moses for serious duty in dealing with Pharaoh, he came back to God with, *"Lord,*

I have never been eloquent. I am slow of speech and tongue" (Exod. 4:10).

Another time he pled to God, *"I speak with faltering lips"* (Exod. 6:30).

And every time God let him off the hook and let brother Aaron do his talking for him.

Speculation: Scholars have spent undue time on the subject and have come up with the possibility that maybe he stuttered. Or maybe he had a speech impediment of some sort. Or maybe he just couldn't translate his cognitive thoughts into intelligible words. Or maybe he was a victim of the old joke "his tongue got in the way of his eye teeth and he couldn't see what he was saying."

Answer: We have no idea.

3. What was the "thorn" in Paul's flesh?

The Bible says, in Paul's words, *"a thorn was given me in the flesh, a messenger of Satan to harass me, to keep me from becoming conceited"* (2 Cor. 12:7). Paul goes on to tell us that three different times he pleaded with the Lord to take it away from him, but the Lord refused and said, *"My grace is sufficient for you"* (2 Cor. 12:9).

Speculation: Scholars and thinkers have been all over this one for centuries. They have come up with physical problems—such as difficulties with the eyes, migraine headaches, malaria, epilepsy, and even a speech problem, such as Moses had (whatever that was). Others think Paul struggled with seriously undefined temptations. But the most interesting is the "thorn" being Alexander, the coppersmith. Paul said, *"Alexander the coppersmith did me great harm. The Lord will repay him according to his deeds"* (2 Tim. 4:14). And that's all he ventures to tell us about the mysterious Alexander.

Answer: We have no idea.

4. Where is the Ark of the Covenant?

The Bible says the ark was a covenant between God and Israel promising good to them if they obeyed him and his laws. He told them how to build it, and inside they put the stone tablets of the Ten Commandments, Aaron's staff that had budded, and a gold jar of manna. It was so holy that once, a man named Uzzah put his hand against it to keep it from toppling over and was immediately struck dead.

Speculation: The ark was passed around from victor to victor over a period of many years. Most historians believe it was destroyed, while some think it is hidden somewhere in the caves or ruins of the Holy Land. The last mention of it in the Old Testament is in 2 Chronicles 35:3, where it says, *"Put the sacred ark in the temple..."* And then, not until Revelation 11:19 is it ever mentioned again, as John writes, *"Then God's temple in heaven was opened and within his temple was seen the ark of his covenant."*

So, this suggests the belief that the Ark of the Covenant was taken up into heaven, and that is the reason it has never been found.

Answer: We have no idea.

And that is the interesting link between these and so many other little mysteries of the Holy Scriptures. We don't always have the full answers, but it is never on matters of great importance. We are told the essential things that matter and may never be told these smaller things of lesser consequence. And that is what keeps our faith alive and interesting and ever fascinating.

O, the infinite wisdom of God!

Jethro

If you grew up in the church and went to Sunday school as a child, there are probably major Bible stories that are just an inherent part of you. They are second nature to you. I know at Olivet, when I was a kid, it was Sunday school every Sunday and Bible school every summer, and I can remember we would take roles and act out some of the really good ones: the Good Samaritan, the Feeding of the Five Thousand, the Crippled Man Being Lowered through the Roof, the Prodigal Son, and on and on. Even with all this, there were many fantastic stories that fell through the cracks, or maybe were just too complicated for our young minds to understand. But sometimes it is one of these lesser-taught narratives that fascinates us at a more adult time in our lives; which takes us to Jethro and his story back in Exodus 18.

Jethro was the priest of Midian, but more importantly, he was the father-in-law of Moses. Jethro had heard all about the escape from Egypt and the parting of the Red Sea and all that God had done for Moses, and one day he shows up in the desert at Moses' camp to return his daughter, Zipporah (Moses' wife) along with her two sons. This is the first we ever hear that apparently Moses had sent Zipporah and his two boys back to her home for their safety while he was dealing with Pharaoh. This was pretty wise of Moses and also pretty nice of Jethro to make the trip and bring his family to him after everything quieted down.

The two men had a wonderful relationship and mutual respect, because Moses went out to meet him and then they went into the tent and Moses told him all about the experiences he had gone through. Jethro was delighted to hear all these stories and was so appreciative of the favor God had shown his son-in-law that he brought a burnt offering and other sacrifices to the Lord, and all was well with this genteel and happy family reunion.

The next day, Moses continued his work while Jethro sat aside and watched him in action. He watched Moses take the seat of judgement among the people and observed how they crowded around him from morning till night, bringing him their problems, large and small, for him to resolve. Jethro saw that this man was the sole judge of all Israel and marveled at how he met with each individual to hear their personal needs and problems. He solved disputes between parties and patiently explained God's law and decrees to them. Jethro was astonished, impressed, and, quite frankly, troubled by what he had witnessed.

After one day of this, Jethro sat with Moses that evening and said to him, "You can't go on like this. This is too much for one man. Listen to me because I'm going to give you some advice. You have got to find capable and trustworthy men in your camp whom you can teach and delegate duties to. God-fearing men you can train to be fair judges, men who won't take a bribe, and then when there is a really tough case they can't handle, let them bring it to you. But you can't continue hearing every voice and every question from every person here. This is just too much strain on one man."

Moses listened and heard the wisdom in Jethro's words and did exactly as he suggested. He was growing as a leader and finding his way in a world that presented problems he never expected. His father-in-law helped put order in his day and gave him a new outlook on who he was and how he should conduct his life.

Well, I can easily see why we were never told this story in Bible school. You really have to be an adult and feel the pressures and burdens of the real world for this tale of Jethro's advice to mean anything at all. But as we live longer in a frightening world of disorder, we realize we need a plan. We need help. We need a Jethro to speak in a fatherly tone to us and guide us, no matter what our age or position in life may be. Jethro was a godly man, and he spoke to his son-in-law out of compassion and concern for his well-being. And after this brief encounter, we are told that Jethro went back to his own country and we never hear from him again in all of Scripture.

What does it mean? What should we glean from it? Well, maybe Jethro was just a good example of a caring and loving father-in-law. Or maybe it is God's way of telling us all we need to slow down sometimes and let other people help instead of trying to do everything ourselves. And then maybe this was actually the voice of God, and Jethro was an emissary bringing Moses a message he needed to hear at this particular moment. Truth be known, if we're open to it, we may remember a Jethro or two in our lives who has had a positive influence over us and set us on a better path. And who knows—there may even be a Jethro or two in our future. Keep your eyes and your hearts open and be aware!

God Is

God is the colors of the wind
He's the sound you hear when everything is silent
He's the voice you feel but never hear
God is the conscience that keeps you up some nights
He's also the peace that lets you sleep the other nights
God is the wisdom you use when you choose right over
   wrong
He's the net that catches you when you choose wrong
   over right
God does not protect you from all sorrows
He sometimes uses them to get your attention
God is the weather, the atmosphere, the attitude of all
   nature
He's an angry volcano; a soft gentle rain
He's sunshine; he's blizzards, scorching and cold
He is everything man cannot do
He can make a person,
Make it rain, make it snow,
He can make the wind blow
God gives all things freely except proof of his existence
   to those who reject him
That proof is in the sight of the beholder
For those who do not believe, no answer is possible

For those who do believe, no answer is necessary
God is the history we never saw
God is the future we can't see
From "In the Beginning" to the final "Amen"
God is the colors of the wind

Grace be with you.

Faith, Hope, and Charity

FAITH

Now faith is the substance of things hoped for, the evidence of things not seen.

—Hebrews 11:1

And if anyone needs a better definition of the word than this, I'm not the man to give it, nor do I know anyone who is. This says it in such an all-encompassing way. And who is this writer of the book of Hebrews who defines our faith so well in a simple sentence? We have no idea. So, let's go on to the next interesting word.

HOPE

We hope it won't rain tomorrow. We hope our team will win. We hope you have a good day. We don't know that any of this will happen, but we hope it will. And then we read about the hope of heaven. The hope of being with God. But aren't we promised heaven and salvation if we believe? Verses such as these, for example, often confuse more than they clarify:

But now, Lord, what do I look for? My hope is in you (Ps. 39:7).

May the God of hope fill you with all joy and peace as you trust in him, so that you may overflow with hope by the power of the Holy Spirit.
—Rom. 15:13).

They may confuse more than clarify until we realize these are two different words. The hope in our everyday language is merely "wishful thinking." But the hope in the Bible is defined as "confident expectation." Christian hope is "firm assurance; trust." I often feel this word is not explained enough to young believers, and I have found that many are reluctant to question its intended meaning. But shout it from the rooftops, the "hope of heaven" is not hoping you're going to heaven. It's *knowing* you're going because you believe, really believe, in Good Friday and Easter and John 3:16!

CHARITY

What if I say to you, "1 Corinthians 13"? You will probably say, "Ah, yeah, the love chapter! Love is patient, love is kind.... Love never fails.... But the greatest of these is love!" We've heard it read at practically every wedding we've ever attended. But the much-revered King James Version of this passage, the version from which most of us have learned all of the Bible verses we know by heart, *never mentions the word love*. "What?" you say to me. "The love chapter is not about love?"

Well, not until you read all the later versions. KJV is all about charity. The word charity shows up nine times in chapter 13, and the translators saw fit to see it as charity = love. The original Greek word was certainly "agape," which means the strongest form of love, but the KJV did not see it that way.

It is so refreshing and thought-provoking to go back and read that translation and read it with our general conception of the word charity. The Scriptures offer so much more to our growth and understanding than we often stop to enjoy or take advantage of. Consider the final verse of this passage that can never be topped:

> *And now abideth faith, hope, charity, these three; but the greatest of these is charity.*
> —1 Corinthians 13:13

And now for a little pop-culture history. In 1955, a singer by the name of Don Cornell had a top-ten hit called "The Bible Tells Me So." More interestingly, it was written, words and music, by the Queen of the Cowgirls, Dale Evans. And I can't read that last verse in 1 Corinthians 13 without these song lyrics from my childhood running wildly through my head:

> *Have faith, hope, and charity*
> *That's the way to live successfully*
> *How do I know?*
> *The Bible tells me so*
>
> *Don't worry 'bout tomorrow*
> *Just be real good today*
> *The Lord is right beside you*
> *He'll guide you all the way*
>
> *Do good to your enemies*
> *And the blessed Lord you'll surely please*
> *How do I know?*
> *The Bible tells me so*

Can you imagine this title and a message this simple and this Christian ever making an appearance on any music chart today?

To quote our old friend Paul, from that same glorious chapter:

When I was a child, I spake as a child, I understood as a child, I thought as a child: but when I became a man, I put away childish things.
　　　　　　　—1 Corinthians 13:11 (King James Version)

To God be the glory.

Judging

To tell one poor ole human being such as you and me not to pass judgment on another poor ole human being is like pouring a bucket of water into the ocean. It just isn't going to make a lot of difference. It's who we are. It's intrinsic in our makeup. It's how we bend. It's our nature to compare people's actions to what we think the norm should be. To compare them to ourselves. To expect more from someone else than we actually expect from ourselves. Ignoring the empathy that we should be trying to obtain is our nature. But it doesn't mean we shouldn't try. Sometimes it is as simple as saying something nice about someone instead of something catty.

Alice Roosevelt Longworth, Teddy's daughter and a renowned Washington hostess, was famous for saying at a social gathering, "If you can't say something good about someone, sit right here by me." We laugh at this because it's funny and also because it's true.

Try thinking of someone you judged too quickly and too harshly on a first impression and then wound up liking after you got to know them better. We can't judge someone when we don't know what is going on inside them.

You may have a quiet, even temperament and cannot possibly understand the feelings of someone who has fire in their blood and is operating every day on a hair-trigger.

You may have been brought up in a good and caring Christian home by attentive parents while someone else you encounter was brought up in an abusive home, underprivileged, ignored, never a mention of God, no church, and with no one to discuss the things that constantly pounded at their mind and conscience. You were brought up loved. They were brought up lacking.

Have you ever experienced a store clerk or a waitress who was a little short with you? A little impatient. Maybe a little rude? We wind up thinking, "What's with him?" "Can't she be in a little better mood?" We've all been guilty of these kinds of thoughts. But we have no idea what their personal circumstances might be. Maybe they feel dead-end in their job. Maybe they're sick. Or maybe their mother or child is sick. Maybe they're more worried about how they are going to pay the electric bill this month than what we want for dessert. Maybe they need some consideration and understanding and forgiveness instead of more judgment.

Why shouldn't we judge? Because we don't have the intelligence to judge. We don't possess the impartiality and wisdom to make unbiased decisions, not without proper time spent in prayer in serious search of the right and effective answer. And what Jesus asks us in the Sermon on the Mount should make us all sit up and take notice:

Why do you look at the speck that is in your brother's eye, but do not notice the log that is in your own eye?
—Matthew 7:3

What Jesus is telling us here is that we should not judge because we are not good enough to judge.

There is an old legend that the ancient Greeks used to hold trials in the dark so the judge and the jury would not be influenced by anything but the facts.

Here is a challenge for all of us. Let's try to remember something critical we have said about someone recently. (Come on. That shouldn't be that hard.) And then let's make a point to say something nice about that same person. Let's counteract a judgment with a compliment. And don't just think it. Actually say it. It's more cleansing and purging that way. I promise we will feel better about that person and we'll feel better about ourselves.

If you judge people, you have no time to love them.
—Mother Teresa

Easter Sunrise

Easter morning. The Lord is risen! The tomb is empty.

Mary Magdalene arrived at the tomb before sunrise, while it was still dark. It was she who saw the stone had been rolled away. It was she who saw Jesus was no longer inside, and she went running to the strength of the twelve she had learned to respect. She ran to Simon Peter and John and poured out her fear of what had happened. When they heard and understood what she was trying to tell them, these two disciples ran together back to the burial place to see for themselves.

> *So, Peter and the other disciple started for the tomb. Both were running but the other disciple outran Peter and reached the tomb first. He bent over and looked at the strips of linen lying there but did not go in. Then Simon Peter, who was behind him, arrived and went into the tomb. He saw the strips of linen lying there, as well as the burial cloth that had been around Jesus' head. The cloth was folded up by itself, separate from the linen. Finally, the other disciple, who had reached the tomb first, also went inside. He saw and believed. (They still did not understand from Scripture that Jesus had to rise from the dead.)*

> —John 20:3–9

This is how John told the story, and if you read it closely, as if reading it for the first time, you will discover there is so much revealed in his telling. We see the character of each of these men. John outran Peter, and when he reached the place, he bent over and looked in and saw the linen strips. But John only *looked* in. He did not enter. Fear of the unknown? Respect for the burial ground? Whatever kept John from entering, we'll never know. But we do know it had zero effect on Peter, because he never stopped. He boldly went inside alone and examined the tomb for himself. Standing in the emptiness of this mausoleum in the dim light of dawn, where a man had recently lay corpse but was now risen from the dead, he showed no fear or alarm. He seemed to be a man in charge, doing a duty that must be done.

I go back to the physical image I carry of Peter that I spoke of in an earlier chapter. And that image is never stronger in my mind than in the scene we have just witnessed of him entering the tomb in search of Jesus' body. He carries such strength in not just entering a burial place with no hesitation, but in the manner in which he moves around like an investigator. He takes in the evidence of the strips and burial cloth and how they were folded and laying separate. He's calm and in control of his emotional faculties, qualities that made him the leader he was and, even more so, would come to be.

This was the Peter whom Jesus called from the fishing boats. This was the man chosen by God himself to serve his only son. This was the pillar of the coming church. The strong, sometimes brash, sometimes wrong, but hard-willed leader, constantly being molded into what God wanted him to be.

All the glory on Easter morning goes to Christ. He is the glory every morning. Our inspiration and Savior every day. But in Peter, this common man, we learn so much about ourselves. There are so many things we can absorb from this man and benefit from his life that will serve us well in our service to the Lord.

A blessed and peaceful Easter Day!

QUESTION FOR THOUGHT

What was the first name of Barabbas, the prisoner freed in exchange for Jesus' execution?

ANSWER

Barabbas's first name, according to many translations of the Bible, was Jesus (Matt. 27:16). Although it was clearly in the original manuscripts, it's believed the name was left out of earlier translations because it was too confusing.

A True Parable at Harris Teeter Grocery

If a survey were taken, and it probably has been, I would imagine the three most famous parables in the Bible are the Prodigal Son, the Lost Sheep, and the Good Samaritan. These stories of Jesus were used to teach and make points of truth and wisdom to anyone in earshot.

The Prodigal Son gives us an insight into the heart of a loving and forgiving father and sets us up for the kind of love we can expect from God himself. This beautiful story holds such a wide charm for all ages and just keeps revealing itself more and more as we grow older. It makes us evaluate ourselves and determine if we have the right stuff when it comes to being the kind of person we know we should be.

The Lost Sheep falls into that category of "hard sayings of Jesus." It isn't always easy for followers who have devoted their lives to being the best they can be, taking all the right paths along the way, to accept the fact that one who is lost until the last moment will get more attention than they will. But it's true, and it is an integral part of our growth as Christians.

And then there is the Good Samaritan. When we first heard it as little kids, our reaction was, *What a nice man to help someone he didn't even know.* Then a few years later, when we were aware of the strained and hostile feelings between

Jews and Samaritans, we thought, *What a caring thing to do for someone who was really an enemy.* And, as more years passed our way, we realized, *This man actually stopped and spent his time and eventually his hard-earned money on a stranger he inherently didn't acknowledge as friendly and maybe even someone who would likely do harm to him if given the chance.* The old onion just keeps getting peeled, and the revelations and deep meanings of this simple story cling on us and won't stop speaking to us. I marvel at how Jesus could address so much to all age groups with one simple tale.

My "Good Samaritan" story is not nearly as good or as deep, but it left me with a chilling yet spiritual feeling the night it happened. We, the whole family, were on vacation at the beach, and I drove into a nearby town one evening after dinner to look for a particular brand of bottled water I like. There is a great Harris Teeter Supermarket there, where we always shop, and at this time of evening, it was uncrowded as I leisurely walked the aisles. In the bottled-water section, I was looking for black raspberry and eventually found the brand I wanted but could not find the flavor anywhere. There was only one other person in the entire aisle, a man, and we kept passing one another, both looking frantically for our items. I finally said aloud, "I'm looking for black raspberry and I don't see it anywhere."

Surprisingly, he said, "That's funny. So am I."

We laughed at that, and in about a minute, he called out from the end of the aisle, "I just found some!"

I walked toward where he was, and as he reached to the very back of a shelf, he pulled out the last remaining six bottles of the elusive black raspberry and said, "Here, you take three and I'll take three."

I said, "No, you found them. You take all of them."

But as he handed me half of the find, he insisted, and said, "No, we'll share."

I thanked this total stranger for his generosity and kindness, knowing we would likely never see one another again in our lives. Just another guy, probably on vacation with his family, as I was, who happened into a grocery store on a quiet Saturday night at the beach. But a few minutes later, as I was rounding the end of another aisle, I came upon a huge display of the very brand of bottled water we had been searching for. There must have been a hundred bottles of black raspberry stacked up over six feet high. I rushed down every aisle to find him to let him know of the treasure I had just happened upon, but he was nowhere to be found. I went to the checkout counters and even ran out into the parking lot to see if I could spot him. But he was gone, and I never saw him again.

We met just for that one moment and we shared. We often share with friends, but it's a different feeling when you share with strangers who have no ulterior motive, no plot, no plan. Just a good, unselfish heart. As I said earlier, not much of a story compared to the Good Samaritan, but a nice experience for a summer night at the beach.

> *The man with two tunics should share with him who has none, and the one who has food should do the same.*
> —Luke 3:11 (words of John the Baptist)

And the same goes for six bottles of black raspberry water.

Just Like Oscar and Felix

So, that guy you don't really care for said something pretty nasty about you a few years ago. You let it go and never approached him about it and, in time, forgave him. And then about a year later, he did it again. You began being pretty annoyed by him and even avoided him at every opportunity without making a scene. But now this! He's done it again, and it's about all you can take. It seems every time you turn around, he's saying something about you that isn't true, and it is just getting more than you can tolerate. You've had it with him. This is the third time now, and you know in your heart you have given him every chance in the world to be a decent human being. You are through with him and want no more of him whatsoever and everyone who knows about it will see it the way you do.

Well, you may not get any argument from me, but then again, I don't really count. Let's see what the rule on this one is.

Then Peter came to Jesus and asked, "Lord, how many times shall I forgive my brother when he sins against me? Up to seven times?"

—Matthew 18:21

Ever wonder why Peter pulled the number seven out of the air? Actually, it wasn't out of the air at all. He got it from his rabbis, who had always taught the book of Amos 1:3–13. It clearly states, more than once, that God will forgive three times and on the fourth, he begins to punish. Peter just wanted to look gracious, so he upped that number three to a seven when asking Jesus this question. But Jesus surprised him, and us, with an answer that has rung sharply through the ages and still gives us all a little jar of reality every time we read it.

Jesus answered, "I tell you, not seven times, but seventy times seven."
—Matthew 18:22

If the math I'm doing in my head doesn't fail me, I think that's 490 times. One person, one human being, one man or woman is going to "sin against me," cause me grief, give me trouble, or bring harm to me four-hundred ninety times? I don't think so. Jesus used a big number to make a point, and it is obvious he means we should forgive as many times as necessary. Not an easy lesson to accept, and not one any of us will probably be successful with, but it certainly is one we should strive for.

I was a huge fan of *The Odd Couple* TV show back in the seventies. I can quote you lines from just about every episode. One of my favorites is called "The Odd Monks." Oscar and Felix decide to go to a local monastery for a rest and retreat. (I have known people who have really done this, and they claim great peace from the experience.) Oscar winds up gambling with other monks. Felix squeals on him, and they are both sent to do penance by working in the kitchen. An addendum to all this is an order of silence. They are not allowed to speak, with the threat of expulsion from the premises if they do. As you can imagine, funny and frustrating situations arise, and they wind up shouting at one another.

The head monk, Brother Ralph, hears them and rushes in the door and catches them causing a disturbance. Having been caught, Oscar hangs his head in shame and says, "I'm sorry. We'll pack up and leave immediately."

Brother Ralph looks at him blankly and says, "Leave? Why are you leaving? We don't punish people for failing around here. We forgive them. Now, clean up and let's go eat breakfast."

What a beautiful lesson to be learned from a television sitcom. A Sunday message right there on a Friday night. And how many times should we be willing to forgive in this manner? Well, as Peter found out, just as many times as needed.

And when you stand praying, if you hold anything against anyone, forgive him, so that your Father in heaven may forgive you.
—Mark 11:25 (words of Jesus)

Election Day

Whether it's local, statewide, or national, it's time to cast your vote of privilege. I trust you know in your heart of hearts exactly how you will mark your ballot. You may claim you're undecided, but I'd be willing to bet you're leaning more one way than the other. You just haven't told anyone which way that may be. Whatever your choice, my sincere wish is that your vote will be blessed and counted.

The Holy Scriptures give us great lessons on most any subject that may be on our minds at any given time, elections included. The most famous vote in the Bible was conducted by Pontius Pilate. He was standing before the people, and custom dictated the release of one prisoner during the Feast of the Passover. The people always decided who that prisoner would be. Pilate, again, extended them that choice by asking not for a secret ballot but by asking for an open vote between Jesus and Barabbas.

Which of the two do you want me to release to you?"
asked the governor.
"Barabbas," they answered.
"What shall I do then with Jesus, who is called Christ?"
Pilate asked.
They all answered, "Crucify him!"

—Matthew 27:21–22

Of course, there was political hanky-panky going on even back then. The chief priests and elders were going through the crowd persuading and telling the people how to vote.

And then there was the time the twelve disciples found themselves to be only eleven. Judas had done himself in by being overcome with guilt, and he left the loyal group one short. They had to hold an election in order to add another disciple. There were qualifications to be considered. They decided it had to be someone who had known Jesus personally. So, the new man had to come from a larger group of "minor" disciples who had traveled with Jesus' troupe and worked closely with him. Two names came up, but they only needed one. And here is a great biblical trivia question: who were the two candidates for disciple number thirteen?

One was a man with three names. Justus. Joseph. Barsabbas. Why three names? I can't say. We're never told. But the other candidate was simply called Matthias. How were they going to do this? A secret ballot among the Eleven? A raise of hands? Well, first they prayed over it, and this was their prayer:

> *Lord, you know everyone's heart. Show us which of these two you have chosen to take over this apostolic ministry, which Judas left to go where he belongs.*
> —Acts 1:24–25

Then they rolled the dice or cast the lots and left it all in God's control. And they felt confident the right man was chosen. And that man was Matthias. His will be done!

On whichever side of the aisle your feelings fall, I think we all could benefit from the behavior and the discipline of the disciples. Take a few moments between now and Election Day and say just one half of the prayer that they prayed:

Lord, you know everyone's heart. Show us which of these two you have chosen.

And then, like the disciples, we'll leave it all in God's control.

This is and always will be God's country, no matter who stands, has stood, or will stand in charge. This has been and always will be our faith. Even in the Old Testament, centuries before the disciples prayed their prayer of trust, Daniel gave us a truth we simply can't ignore.

Praise be to the name of God forever and ever;
Wisdom and power are his.
He changes times and seasons;
He sets up kings and deposes them.
He gives wisdom to the wise
And knowledge to the discerning.
He reveals deep and hidden things;
He knows what lies in darkness,
And light dwells with him.
I thank and praise you, O God of my fathers
You have given me wisdom and power.
You have made known to me what we asked of you.
—Daniel 2:20–23

And he will. He will make known to us what we ask of him. He's done it before and he'll do it again. In his way. In his time. His will be done!

Joining the Church

Do you remember the day you first joined a church? Maybe you've been a member of a number of different congregations and even denominations. And if so, I'm sure every one of them is very special in your mind. But that first one—that one you came to not with a letter of transfer but with a confession of faith—that is the one that is probably the most memorable to you. That's the one that holds a place in your heart like no other.

We had a very touching and moving experience in the field behind our church where we held Sunday-morning services during that strange and uncomfortable period when we couldn't legally go indoors. On a beautiful autumn morning, five teenagers from our congregation joined the church, and it was a moment I think none of us will soon forget. They each stood with our minister and answered questions concerning their dedication to God, and then each one went to the microphone and read their personal statement of faith. Each one gave a scripturally correct assessment, in their own words, of what they believe and why they believe it. It put a smile on all our faces and a warmth in our hearts that defied every media image of fourteen- and fifteen-year-olds that we are accustomed to seeing and hearing about. Our minister, Lee Thomas, asked blessings on each of them individually, and then we all stood and gave our thanks for their commitment and loyalty by repeating together the words of the Apostles' Creed.

One of the five was a daughter of our minister. Two of the five were a son and daughter of two of our fellow church families. The other two were my grandchildren. But I was proud of all five of them for publicly doing what they did and how they did it. When it was all over, I said a special prayer for the ten parents of those teens. It was they who have brought them to church each Sunday morning all their lives. It was those moms and dads who saw they were dressed and present when it might have been easier to leave them in bed sometimes. It was they who made the effort to see they had a constant dose of the environment of a church life at the beginning of each week. Those parents did it the right way. I had to think to myself, they did it the Hannah way.

Hannah's story in 1 Samuel, first chapter, is one we all can benefit from knowing. She was a young woman who wanted nothing more than to have a son of her own. Just how much she wanted this child is plainly stated in her personal prayer to God:

> *O Lord Almighty, if you will only look upon my misery and remember me and not forget me but give me a son, then I will give him to the Lord for all the days of his life.*
> —1 Samuel 1:11

In time, Hannah finally conceived and gave birth to a son. She named him Samuel, and she never forgot the promise she had made to God. As soon as the boy was weaned, she took him to the temple at Shiloh, to the old priest, Eli. As she presented her baby boy to Eli, she said to him:

*I prayed for this child and the Lord has granted me
what I asked of him. So now I give him to the Lord.
For his whole life he will be given over to the Lord.*
—1 Samuel 1: 27

And Samuel grew up *in* the temple, the house of the
Lord. This is a much bigger "dose of the environment of a
church life" than any of us ever had in mind, but it does tend
to offer a good life lesson. It was God's will that Samuel
would become a great prophet of Israel. His background and
education were rooted in the temple life, and his learning
years were nurtured in God's love and teachings. Children
need to be in the right atmosphere and settings to receive the
proper influence. We can't expect them to know the Bible,
to inherently have a true understanding of right and wrong,
or to have the strength to stand up and say it, if we fail to
give them the opportunity of a church life and a church family.

None of us ever had or ever will have the courage of
Hannah. We won't give our children up completely, but we
can give them a taste of what's right for them. And for that
I commend those ten parents. Blessings to each of you and
your sweet and lovely children and to all of you who have
done the same down through the years.

*One generation will commend your works to another;
they will tell of your mighty acts.*
—Psalm 145:4

It's a Gift

I like reading surveys. I realize they are not foolproof and are only an essence of what the truth may be, but I have found that they do often give us an insight into what may be on people's minds. I have always wanted to be a part of these surveys, but I have only been asked once. I was stopped, many years ago, as I was exiting a hotel in a foreign city and asked about my television-viewing habits. It was frivolous and silly but kind of fun. But I'd really like to be involved in one that means something. And here is one that certainly does!

The Arizona Christian University Cultural Research Center conducted a survey on salvation and how you get it. Here are a few statements they asked two thousand people to mark true or false:

You consider yourself to be a Christian, and when you die you will go to heaven only because you have confessed your sins and have accepted Jesus Christ as your savior.

Only one third agreed.

If you are generally good and do enough good things during your life, you will "earn" a place in heaven.

Half agreed with this.

Having faith matters more than which faith you have.

Two thirds agreed with this one.

I can think of at least seven different times in the New Testament when Jesus told someone that their faith had saved them, healed them, or made them whole, and I'm sure you can, too. And if they want it said in a way that is clear even to the those with the smallest of faith and biblical knowledge, they should check out the way our old friend Paul says it:

> *For it is by grace you have been saved, through faith—*
> *and this is not from yourselves, it is the gift of God—*
> *not by works, so that no one can boast.*
> —Ephesians 2:8–9

In summing up, this survey said, "With American adults increasingly rejecting biblical answers to key questions of life, it is little surprise that current views of sin and salvation are increasingly void of biblical understanding."

And with that said, I had to rethink what I was feeling about some of these uninformed participants, because it goes even deeper.

About fifteen years ago, I attended a Sunday-morning church service during which an ordained minister stood in the pulpit and for twenty minutes disparaged and trashed the words of Jesus in John 14:6: *I am the way and the truth and the life. No one comes to the Father except through me.*

I, along with others that morning, sat there shocked, bewildered, and angry. The shock and bewilderment wore off, and after the service, I approached him. Needless to say, I didn't change his mind and he didn't change mine. Turned out he was a universalist who not only believes everyone is going to heaven no matter what their faith is, but also that there is no hell.

I learned from that moment to not be shocked by what some Christian people believe when that is what is being preached from too many pulpits. It makes me thankful for the minister we cherish and love so much at Olivet. We are blessed and thankful to have him.

And one final thought I'd love to offer to those out there who are so far from the Holy Scriptures in what they believe about Jesus and heaven and how to get there. This simple formula is mine and is stated as clearly as I know how:

Grace + Faith + Nothing else = Salvation

But in today's complicated world, I honestly think this is too simple for many folks to grasp. They think there should be some sort of burden on them, some heavy lifting they have to do to get God's attention, some great task they have to perform, some pain and strain they have to endure. That's where the *+ Nothing else* part kicks in.

It's a gift. Simply accept it and live happily ever after!

Constant Prayer

I had a little computer problem recently, which is not unusual for me. There must be a covey of little demons living in the deep recesses of all my electronic devices just waiting to see what havoc they can shower on me at any given time. Usually, when this happens, I call a technician or one of my sons or one of my grandchildren. But this time I was determined to fix it myself. The solution consisted, in part, of entering a new password for my desktop, my iPhone, and my iPad. The first two transitioned just fine, but I worked off and on for eighteen hours and the iPad would just not cooperate. I tried entering the new password. I tried re-entering the old one. I counted those little dots dozens of times to make sure I had the right amount of numbers and letters in my new code word. I tried everything imaginable right up to throwing it against the wall to get its attention. (Not really, but it did cross my mind a couple of times.)

After all this hassle and worry, I finally said out loud, "Lord, I'm going to try to do this just one more time. It is all in your hands because I don't know what else to do." I promise you every word I'm telling you here is true. As soon as I put in the password and hit "Enter," a flood of messages and emails that had been blocked for days opened up and started rushing through in perfect order. The iPad was healed, and

I had witnessed another small miracle that came from depending on God.

I have always been a praying person, as I'm sure every one of you have been, too. But I honestly think sometimes we save too much of the power of prayer for the big stuff. I know in my heart we all pray daily for healings for family and friends. We pray for resolutions to world crises. We pray for safe travel. For relationships. For our church. For our country. For spiritual and moral guidance. But too often, and I speak now just for myself, I tend not to bother the good Lord with the small things that might make me seem selfish and wrapped up in my own comfort. And I sincerely think that is what this little computer problem was all about. It was God reminding me that he is in everything. He is there for everything that we need. Nothing is too small for his attention, and nothing is too insignificant in our minds that we don't need his help in solving or maintaining it.

Remember the Parable of the Persistent Widow (Luke 18)? There was an unjust judge who didn't care about God or the people in his jurisdiction. He was incompetent and no good. A widow kept approaching him, begging for him to give justice to her against an adversary. (We are never told any particulars of the case.) She was relentless and persistent in her never-ending pleas and visits until the judge just finally said to himself, "This woman is driving me up the wall. I'll give her justice to get rid of her because she is wearing me out."

Jesus tells this parable to his disciples and says, "If a judge who has no love and respect for God, who is unfit and uncaring, can in the end give justice, think what justice a loving Father will bring to his chosen ones who cry out to him day and night. I tell you they will get justice and quickly."

Apart from me you can do nothing.
—John 15:5

Praying for small things does not offend God. It shows him, and more importantly it shows us, just how much we depend on him. So, it's okay to pray for a parking space close to the entrance at Lowe's. It may not be the one you have in mind, but it will be better than if you don't pray at all. And when the kitchen stress starts to build while preparing that big meal for company, don't ever think you're bothering him. Stop and say a word to him and ask for his help. He has big shoulders and he's told us he cares. He wants us to be comfortable and happy, but most of all he wants us to be reliant on him. He wants our trust in everything we do, large and small.

Don't be anxious about anything, but in everything, by prayer and petition...present your requests to God.
—Philippians 4:6

Father's Day

We celebrated Mother's Day and have reviewed its history, so as to not slight half our parents, it's only fitting we give equal time to our fathers.

It is generally accepted that Father's Day found its creation in the great northwest city of Spokane, Washington. A young lady by the name of Sonora Louise Smart Dodd was sitting in a church service on a spring Sunday morning listening to a sermon on Mother's Day. During this particular service, she struggled to hear all the words the minister was saying as her mind kept wondering why there was never a proper Father's Day. And Sonora had every reason to feel this affinity for fathers because of her special adoration and love for her own. Sonora was one of six children, and at a very early age, her mother had died and left the rearing of her and her siblings to this man she so admired.

Sonora's father was William Jackson Smart, a Civil War veteran who had lost his wife in childbirth and raised this house full of children all by himself with never a complaint or a grumble. He was the finest man she had ever known, and she wanted the world to know how much she loved and cherished him for all he had done for his family.

It wasn't just a childish whim, because Sonora was twenty-seven years old and married when she got this inspiring idea. She knew Anna Jarvis was making this happen for all the mothers in the world, so why couldn't she make the same happen for the fathers? The year was 1909, and her first course of action was to draw up a petition recommending a national Father's Day. She got the endorsement of the Spokane Ministerial Association and the local Young Men's Christian Association (YMCA). The city of Spokane celebrated the first Father's Day just one year later, on June 19, 1910.

Although this first one was just a local observance, it set a fire in this caring and ambitious daughter to take it to higher levels. Just six years later, in 1916, President Woodrow Wilson gave his approval for a day set aside to honor fathers. The concept grew, and by 1924, President Calvin Coolidge gave public praise for the day and all it stood for. All this time, a Sunday in June was being acknowledged, but nothing official was happening the way Sonora Dodd had hoped for. It wasn't until 1966 that President Lyndon Johnson signed a proclamation making the third Sunday in June Father's Day. And then, not until 1972 was it completely official, when President Richard Nixon declared it a permanent national observance day.

A daughter may outgrow your lap but she will never outgrow your heart.

—Unknown

And here is the sweetest part of the story. Sonora Louise Smart Dodd lived to finally see all this happen. She was publicly honored for her accomplishment at the World's Fair in Spokane in 1974. Over a period spanning sixty-three years, she saw her seed of an idea, from that long-ago church service, become a national monument for all fathers in the US, and especially for her own cherished father, who had made such a lasting impression on her heart. Mrs. Dodd died in 1978 at the age of ninety-six.

He will turn the hearts of the fathers to their children,
and the hearts of the children to their fathers.
—Malachi 4:6

I think it's interesting to note that the first Father's Day church service, on June 19, 1910, in Spokane, was held in the Old Centenary Presbyterian Church, now known as Knox Presbyterian Church. The sermon was by Dr. Conrad Bluhm, and on that Sunday morning, a new tradition was begun. The young women's group, called the Alphas, passed out a red rose to each father who entered the church. Then baskets of red and white roses were passed among the congregation, and all those present were invited to take a red rose if their father was alive or a white rose if deceased. That beautiful tradition of wearing a rose on Father's Day lives on today, though no longer widely observed.

After the service that morning, Sonora Dodd, traveling in a two-horse carriage and carrying her infant son in her arms, delivered gifts to shut-in fathers.

And in closing, here is a remembrance from the most popular and oft-read parable in all Scripture, honoring the love and passion of a forgiving and caring father.

But while he was still a long way off, his father saw
him and was filled with compassion for him; he ran to
his son, threw his arms around him and kissed him.
—Luke 15:20

To all the dads who always held our hands and had our backs, Happy Father's Day.

Homesick

Here's another old family story from our Reid clan. Our grandparents lived in Springhill, about a thirty-minute drive from our house, in an old stone, pre-Civil War home that still stands out there on the one-lane country road to this day. At the time of this particular incident, sometime in the late forties, they still had no phone service out that far in the county. The closest phone was behind the counter of an old country store more than two miles away. The summer my brother, Harold, was about eight or nine years old, he got it in his head he wanted to go out to Grandma and Granddaddy's house and spend a week. No amount of "Are you sure?" and "A whole week?" would dissuade him in the least. So, Mom and Dad put his trusty old Schwinn bicycle in the trunk of the car, along with his ball glove and cap pistols, and dropped him off, and he waved a vigorous goodbye to them from the front porch.

All was well in heart and mind until bedtime. In order for him to get to his bedroom, he had to walk through the parlor, and there atop an old grand piano sat a framed picture of our mother. Sadness, homesickness, and nostalgia hit him so hard and so suddenly right in the stomach, he went to bed but never slept a second. The next morning, he was up early with a master plan swirling in his mind. He jumped on his bike and rode like a hard wind, pedaling for all he was worth, toward that little country store. He called home and poured out his heart. Now, if our mom had answered the phone, she would have probably used this as a teaching moment and lovingly cajoled him into staying another night or two, and all would have been well and this story would have a different ending. But our dad answered, and being the old softie he was, within the hour, Harold's bike and suitcase were in the back of the car, and he and Dad were heading back home to Staunton.

I have felt the pangs of homesickness, and I'm guessing you have, too. It is a lonesome agony that won't let go of you. You get things in your mind that won't pass through, and there is no peace with the longings that you just can't shake. Many things can make us homesick. A picture, like that one on the piano, a song, the smell of a certain food cooking, simply being alone, remembering a favorite time in life or a favorite person. And those feelings have been with us for centuries. Even King David had them.

Israel was at war with the Philistines. So, what else is new? It seems these two nations were always fighting one another. This time, the Philistines had set up a stronghold around the town of Bethlehem. King David was camped out in the cave of Adullam when three of his "mighty men" came to check on him. In the course of their conversation, in a moment of reflection and, yes, homesickness, David's mind went back to the better times of his childhood. Bethlehem was his hometown, the place he had grown up and tended sheep on his father's farm. And in a weak and aching moment of longing, the king said, "Oh, that someone would get me a drink of water from the well near the gate of Bethlehem." You might even say he was thinking out loud, but these three faithful warriors, Josheb, Eleazar, and Shammah, took to heart the request of their king.

They left him, and 2 Samuel 23:16 tells us they *broke through the Philistine lines, drew water from the well near the gate of Bethlehem, and carried it back to David.* These were mighty men, loyal men who were at the call of their commander-in-chief's smallest, most impulsive wish. More love and respect you could not ask for.

But when they returned with the water, David refused to drink it. Instead, he poured it out on the ground before the Lord and said, "Far be it from me, O Lord, to do this. Is it not the blood of men who went at the risk of their lives?"

It looks like David had as much love and respect for these soldiers as they did for him. As much as he wanted to taste a sip of that sweet nectar from his youth, he sacrificed it in honor of the jeopardy and endangerment these men had put themselves in at his whim. Although he was suffering from a homesickness for more peaceful times in his life, he poured it out before the Lord. Is it any wonder that God is quoted in Acts 13:22: *I have found David, son of Jesse, a man after my own heart; he will do everything I want him to do.*

If you have never felt that forlorn feeling in the pit of your stomach, I hope you never will. But what David and Harold and some of you and I have felt is expressed beautifully by my favorite old poet, Edgar A. Guest (1881–1959). Here are just a few opening lines from his aptly titled poem "Homesick."

> It's tough when you are homesick in a strange and dis-
> tant place;
> It's anguish when you're hungry for an old familiar
> face.

*And yearning for the good folks and the joys you used
    to know,*
*When you're miles away from friendship, is a bitter
    sort of woe.*

Near to the Heart

You don't know what you have until it's gone.

This old saying can apply to just about anything you want it to. I've heard it used about past loves. About money. About a way of life. A person. A job. Youth. Security. Health. Even a good era that you enjoyed living in. The old folks of every generation have and will talk about how much better the old times were than the times that surround them now. It isn't always true, but I think in our minds we like to believe it is.

We all have been through quite a bit of that, having experienced the year 2020. We look back on the pandemic and the hardships and wonder how we ever made it. Lives changed. Habits changed. The essential ways of living erupted and we found ourselves thrown topsy-turvy, higgledy-piggledy, and pell-mell. Jobs were lost and may never be found again. Workplaces closed and people worked from home. Schools closed and students worked from their bedrooms. Zoom meetings became the norm. Even doctors began seeing patients by computer appointments. Nobody shopped in the malls. Eat-in restaurants were shutting down, and if they didn't have a drive-thru window on the side of their kitchen, they had to become a take-out and delivery service overnight. More and more, we were eating at home. No movie theaters. No concerts. No ball games. People were inventing drive-by birthday parties. Graduation ceremonies were cancelled. Weddings were postponed. And funerals were little more than a notice and an announcement on a newspaper page.

All this created a tension and an uneasiness that permeated throughout the population. Politics got involved. Tempers flared. Opinions between family members and friends got heated on how best to handle the prevention and spread of this demon germ. It became a youth versus age issue. It became a liberal versus conservative dispute. There seemed to be no end to the problems and division it would cause, and no one wanted to listen to anyone else's solution to the matter. It was a war of words and action that separated decent-thinking people. No one and no place were exempt from its reach. Even churches were being split. Some stayed open to prove they could and were criticized for putting the faithful at risk. Those who closed their doors and took precautions were accused of being too easily scared, and the strength of their faith was questioned. Just more proof that there is no easy answer. Even going to church can be hard.

We have no idea what church might look like in the future. Whether two months or two years from now, we can only hope it will someday get back to normal. Back to the way it was before March of 2020. No restrictions. No masks. No fears. No distancing and bumping elbows. Just a happy and safe place to be with family and friends who share a love of Christ and of one another. But when that happens, and let's continue to pray it will, keep in mind there will always be aspects of being in church that are hard and personal. Even when the pandemic scare is over, all the other things that plague our very souls, our sanity, and our deepest feelings will not just be solved and healed overnight.

When you go and take your place in the pew, never think you're the only one there who has a problem eating away at your heart. Never let a ready smile from the person sitting across the aisle allow you to think they wouldn't understand the turmoil your conscience is causing inside your chest. Never let a warm and friendly greeting make you think that person doesn't understand heartache and loss. Church, on its best days, can be hard for us all at times, and particularly so if we carry too much inside.

First, take it to the Lord and then share a little of that burden with those fellow Christians who are more schooled in life than you often give them credit for. Do everything in your power to not make church hard for anyone, especially yourself. It should be a place of refuge and peace. A place to take a deep breath and be quiet with God, away from the world for a few moments every week. Church is a family that cares when you aren't there, that checks on you when you're sick, that helps you when you need a hand, and listens, without judgement, when you want to get something off your heart.

> *For where two or three are gathered together in my name, there am I in the midst of them.*
> —Matthew 18:20

There is a place of quiet rest
Near to the heart of God
A place where sin cannot molest
Near to the heart of God
> "Near to the Heart of God"
> —Cleland Boyd McAfee

Just One Thing

Everyone has probably played that game of "If your house was on fire and you could save just one thing, what would it be?" It's a tragic thing to think about, and hardly a fun topic to consider, but it makes a good point. I remember reading many years ago about a family that lived in a castle on a hillside in California who got caught in one of their raging wildfires. The flames were closing in on the house, and there were few precious minutes to save anything. The daughter of an Iranian oilman owned the home, and as she rushed through the rooms a final time, she gathered what she could and ran frantically out the door. In the safe glow of daylight, she found that the two things she had saved, in the emotion of the moment, were a handful of jewelry and a pair of Elvis's army fatigues she had bought at a celebrity auction. Don't know if any of us would have done any better or worse, considering the state of mindlessness we would be in at the time.

I want to give you an opportunity to play a form of this game without the pressure of fire and loss staring you in the face. I'm going to give you ten things, in alphabetical order, that we may cherish and regard in our daily lives as very important to us. Some are intangible while others are things we can touch. Then I'm going to challenge you to put them in the order of importance to you personally. Take your time.

Think about each item listed here. Talk to yourself about what you feel is most dear to you and your life, and rate it on a scale from one to ten. The X-Factor is open-ended. You fill that one in, since I don't know what it will be for you.

Family
Friends
God
Health
Hobbies
Home
Job
Money
Romantic Relationship
X-Factor

1.

2.

3.

4.

5.

6.

7.

8.

9.

10.

In the 1991 movie *City Slickers*, Billy Crystal (Mitch) and Jack Palance (Curly) are riding horses, side by side, and having a philosophical conversation about life.

> *Curly:* Do you know what the secret of life is? (Raises his index finger)
>
> *Mitch:* Your finger?
>
> *Curly:* One thing. Just one thing. You stick to that one thing and all the rest doesn't matter.
>
> *Mitch:* But what is that one thing?
>
> *Curly:* That's what you have to find out.

Maybe this little "fill-in-the-blanks" challenge will help you determine what that one thing is for you. That one thing, at the top of your list, that is so important to you that all the rest doesn't matter. It's a game you'll want to play alone so you can be brutally honest with yourself. In doing so, you may learn more about the way you think and feel than you are willing to admit to a roomful of game players. Keep in mind that whatever is number one is what controls you. Number one determines who you are and how you feel about the other nine. Good luck and enjoy some time looking inside and getting to know yourself.

Independence Day

It's flag-waving weekend for all America. A time to remember and celebrate our religious freedom and our independence as one nation, under God, indivisible, with liberty and justice for all. With all glory going to him, here are a few interesting facts that, when looked at a little closer, make us thankful our nation has been established under the sovereign hand of God.

This story of God's intervention in America's freedom has been attributed to a couple of different battles in World War II. Frankly, when and where it happened is not really the story, but that it happened at all is the glory we garner from it. This is the most popular version handed down in time.

General George Patton, in December of 1944, was getting his troops ready for what would be the bloodiest battle in American history, the Battle of the Bulge. Dark days of clouds and heavy rain were stymying all his preplanning and preparation. The general called in his Third Army chaplain, Colonel James O'Neil, and told him he needed a prayer to clear the weather before he could move his army. O'Neil went back to his quarters and searched through official prayer books for one concerning the weather. He found nothing and subsequently decided to pen an original prayer of his own. He took the freshly written prayer back to Patton, read it to him, and waited for his reaction. His reaction was to order Chaplain O'Neil to have 250,000 wallet-sized copies of his prayer printed and distributed to every man in the Third. This was Patton's prayer:

Almighty and most merciful Father, we humbly beseech Thee, of Thy great goodness, to restrain these immoderate rains with which we have had to contend. Grant us fair weather for Battle. Graciously hearken to us as soldiers who call upon Thee that, armed with Thy power, we may advance from victory to victory, and crush the oppression and wickedness of our enemies and establish Thy justice among men and nations.

The clouds lifted, the rain stopped for the next six days, and Patton's army "advanced to victory." And God smiled on America again.

———

During the Battle of Monongahela, George Washington came to fight, but with a severe headache and high fever. Then, to complicate matters, he had not one but two horses shot out from under him. That not being enough for one battle, he also had four bullets put through his coat and his hat shot off his head. But he still came through it all to be our first president!

———

Ford's Theatre was not the first time Abraham Lincoln was the target of someone's twisted plan. In August of 1864, a sniper took a shot at him and knocked his stovepipe hat off his head.

———

In Russia, May 10, 2005, someone threw a live hand grenade at George W. Bush. The pin had been pulled, but it didn't explode because it was wrapped in a red handkerchief that kept the safety lever from detaching.

A man opened fire on the White House in an attempt on Bill Clinton's life and was tackled and held by a group of tourists.

Lynette "Squeaky" Fromme, of the Manson family, tried to take a shot at Gerald Ford on September 5, 1975. She was in a crowd along a rope line where he was shaking hands in Sacramento and standing only two feet from him. She raised the Colt .45 automatic and pulled the trigger not knowing she had to first slide a bullet into the chamber.

Teddy Roosevelt was giving a speech in Milwaukee in October of 1912. Before he began, he had folded his prepared notes and put them in his breast pocket. During his address, he was shot in the chest, but the pages slowed the bullet enough to make it only a wound. He showed the bloody sheets of paper to his audience and apologized for having to shorten his talk a little. Ignoring his staff, who begged him to stop, he finished his speech before going to the hospital.

And then there was President Andrew Jackson, who was attending the funeral of a friend when a madman named Richard Lawrence walked up to him and pulled the trigger. The gun jammed and Lawrence pulled a second one from his pocket, but it misfired as well. At this point, angry and annoyed, Jackson proceeded to beat the man over the head with his cane. (Hickory, I presume.)

Miracles didn't just happen in the Bible, and miracles don't just happen in history. They're happening all around us every moment we live and breathe. Let's all keep our hearts open and watch for the miracles that are happening in our lives every day.

There was a sarcastic and tongue-in-cheek expression going around the world as far back as 1849 that can still be heard and read: "A special Providence watches over children, drunks, and the United States."

And that Providence is the hand of the Lord!

Happy Fourth of July!

153 Fish

After the Resurrection, Peter's mission was just beginning. He had had three full years of on-the-job training with Jesus in the flesh, but now he was looking at about thirty-two years of his own mission before him. Traditional history tells us Peter was just a few years older than Jesus and that he lived to be around sixty-eight years of age. Much happened to him after the Ascension, when his personal ministry began, but for today, let's look at Peter's involvement in the Christian story during those forty days between the Resurrection and the Ascension.

Peter witnessed Jesus on that first Easter night when Jesus came through the walls of the house where ten of the disciples were hiding. (Judas and Thomas were not there.) He was there exactly a week later, on Sunday night, in the same house, when Jesus materialized in front of eleven of the disciples and confronted Thomas for doubting him. John tells us Peter and the other disciples were privy to many miracles that were never written down. But this next famous story was written down, and it reinstated and empowered Peter to become the fearless spokesman that he would become for God's future church.

The setting was the shore of the Sea of Tiberias. Peter, Thomas, Nathaniel, James, John, and two other unnamed disciples decided to take a boat out and go fishing. They fished all night long, and come dawn, they had caught absolutely nothing. In the dim gray light of early morning, they could see a man standing on the beach they didn't recognize. This man yelled out to them and asked, "Have you caught any fish?"

"No," was the simple answer from all seven of them.

"Throw the net out on the right side of the boat and you'll catch some," the stranger on the shore shouted back.

Tired, weary, and discouraged, they did and caught so many fish in their net they weren't able to haul it back onto the boat. It was then John said to Peter, as he pointed to the man standing near the water, "It is the Lord!" At this, Peter jumped into the water and rushed toward him while the others brought the boat and the fish closer to the shore. And there sat Jesus, in front of a fire, with fish and bread waiting for them. He told Peter to bring some of the fish they had just caught, so Peter ran back to the boat and dragged the net behind him that was full of 153 large fish. Jesus' simple invitation was, "Come and have breakfast."

After they had eaten, Jesus asked Peter three times if he loved him. Each time Peter answered in the positive, Jesus told him to "feed my sheep." Not much mystery here. Jesus gave Peter three opportunities to redeem his three sins of denial from that courtyard while Jesus was standing trial. Then, he was telling him to go out and take the Word to the world.

The mystery, if you want mystery, remains in the 153 fish that were caught that morning. Theologians and scholars galore have scratched their heads over this one for centuries. They have argued numerous mathematical calculations that border on the edge of sanity, but none seem to satisfy why the number of fish was recorded. The Scriptures never explain it, so it could be as simple as the disciples counted them out so that they could divvy them up equally among themselves. Or, maybe you'll like the theory of Biblical historian Jerome, who lived in the fourth century. He said at the time that there were 153 kinds of fish known to the world, and this was symbolic that someday people of all nations would be gathered together to Jesus Christ. And when they all came, the church—the net—would hold them and not break.

To add to Jerome's point, I ask you to consider the fact that Peter ran back into the water and it was *he* who brought all the fish to shore. He, who would open up salvation to all nations, brought all the fish and laid them at Jesus' feet. Peter, who would stand on that mountain in Galilee alongside the other ten and hear the risen Jesus give the Great Commission:

> *Go ye therefore, and teach all nations, baptizing them in the name of the Father, and of the Son, and of the Holy Ghost: Teaching them to observe all things whatsoever I have commanded you: and, lo, I am with you always, even unto the end of the world. Amen.*
>
> —Matthew 18:19–20

Peter's mission was stirring and was about to be launched. Christ had just proclaimed him to be the shepherd of the people. There is so much more to know about this man called Peter, but for now, I'll leave you with Peter's own words from the closing of his second book "To him be glory both now and forever. Amen."

QUESTION FOR THOUGHT

John says disciple Nathaniel was on the boat. You may know him by another name. It is the common belief that _____ and Nathaniel were the same person.

ANSWER

Bartholomew. The first three Gospels never mention Nathaniel, while John never mentions Bartholomew. With much historical cross-referencing, it is the consensus among biblical scholars and researchers that these two disciples were the same person. A number of the disciples had more than one name:

Matthew/Levi
Judas, the son of James/Thaddaeus/Lebbaeus
Thomas/Didymus
Simon/Peter/Simon Peter/Cephas/Simeon

Fanny J.

Probably the three most famous songwriters in American history are Stephen Foster, Irving Berlin, and Fanny J. Crosby. Depending on the sources you use, Fanny Crosby is credited with writing anywhere from three thousand to nine thousand songs in her lifetime. Even taking the lowest number, it is phenomenal. We can cover only a handful of her most famous hymns here.

"Pass Me Not, O Gentle Saviour"
Pass me not, O gentle Saviour / Hear my humble cry
While on others Thou art calling / Do not pass me by

She wrote folk songs, popular songs, patriotic songs, and, of course, classic hymns in her era (1820–1915).

"All the Way My Saviour Leads Me"
All the way my Saviour leads me / What have I to ask
*   beside?*
Can I doubt His tender mercy / Who through life has
*   been my guide?*

She was a school teacher by profession. She taught English grammar and Roman and American history.

"To God Be the Glory"
Praise the Lord, Praise the Lord / Let the earth hear
His voice

Praise the Lord, Praise the Lord / Let the people rejoice
O come to the Father through Jesus the Son
And give Him the glory / Great things He hath done

She wrote a few of her songs alone but most often collaborated with other writers. When she did this, she always took the role of lyricist even though she was proficient on the guitar and the piano.

"I Am Thine, O Lord"
I am thine, O Lord, I have heard Thy voice / And it
told Thy love to me
But I long to rise in the arms of faith / And be closer
drawn to Thee

Fanny J. Crosby was blind from the time she was six weeks old. When once asked about her blindness, she said, "If perfect earthly sight was offered to me tomorrow, I would not accept it. I might not have sung hymns to the praise of God if I had been distracted by the beautiful and interesting things about me. And when I get to heaven, the first face that shall ever gladden my sight will be that of my Savior."

"Jesus, Keep Me Near the Cross"
In the cross, in the cross / Be my glory ever
Till my raptured soul shall find / Rest beyond the river

Fanny and Bing Crosby were distantly related. Rev. Thomas Crosby of Boston was a second-great-grandfather of Fanny and a fifth-great-grandfather of Bing.

"Praise Him, Praise Him"
Praise Him, Praise Him / Jesus our blessed Redeemer
Sing O earth, His wonderful love proclaim
Hail Him, hail Him / Highest archangels in glory
Strength and honor give to his Holy name

She was married to a blind music teacher, Alexander van Alstyne Jr., and they had one daughter, Frances, who died in infancy of typhoid fever. The death of their child inspired the writing of this hymn. Although not one of her most famous ones, Fanny always said it was her favorite of all her compositions.

"Safe in the Arms of Jesus"
Safe in the arms of Jesus / Safe on his gentle breast
There by His love o'er shaded / Sweetly my soul shall rest

Fanny often wrote six or seven songs a day. Before writing each one, she would have a prayer. During her career, she used dozens of pseudonyms because publishers balked at using so many songs for their hymnals and songbooks under one name. Some names we know; some we may never know.

"Tell Me the Story of Jesus"
Tell me the story of Jesus / Write on my heart every word
Tell me the story most precious / Sweetest that ever was heard

Fanny J. Crosby died on February 12, 1915, at ninety-four years old. As the Scriptures say of Abraham, she "died at a good old age" (Gen. 25:8). She was buried in Bridgeport, Connecticut, and her family, at her request, placed a small, modest stone over her grave that simply read:

Aunt Fanny—She hath done what she could

Forty years later, on May 1, 1955, the public who loved her erected a huge vertical stone over five feet tall at her gravesite with the words of the first stanza to maybe her best and most loved hymn of all. The title alone gives me chills, and the words never fail to give me tears. It was my mother's favorite hymn, and as I grow older, it's becoming mine.

"Blessed Assurance"
Blessed Assurance, Jesus is mine / O what a foretaste of glory divine
Heir of salvation, Purchase of God / Born of His spirit, washed in His blood

FANNY J. CROSBY

She hath done what she could
—Mark 14:8

One Defining Moment

We spend our entire lives doing the things we think are right. We try to be the person we should be every hour of every day. We want our children and all our families to be proud of us, so we stay aware of how we are handling ourselves in every difficult situation. But then it happens. We let our guard down for just a moment and someone is watching. Someone is seeing us at our worst. "Without makeup" is the way it's expressed today. And the very sad fact of it all is that you can't put the glue back in the tube. Once it's out there, it's going to stick.

All of you adamant sports fans and history buffs of the sports world will know the name of Bill Buckner. Ah, yes, I can see some of you smiling already. But for those still in the dark, let me shine a little light on who this man was and why his name is so famous in his field. Bill Buckner was a first baseman for the Boston Red Sox, and that is where he was standing when his defining moment in history befell him. It was the World Series of 1986. The score was tied in the tenth inning. Mookie Wilson of the New York Mets was at the plate with a runner on second base. He hit a slow ground ball down the first base line, and as Bill Buckner reached down to scoop it up, it went through his legs, rolling into right field. Ray Knight, the runner on second, scored, and the World Series rings went to the Amazin' Mets. And poor Bill Buckner found his notorious and infamous place in baseball history. Ask any zealous fan of the sport and they can describe this embarrassing moment in detail.

What they probably can't or won't describe to you are the many wonderful and brilliant moments in Buckner's twenty-one-year baseball career. No one remembers all the grounders he fielded perfectly at first all those years, the full-stretch snags he reached out and got, the line drives coming hard and fast off a bat at close range. They won't remember the year he led the league in doubles, the two seasons he finished in the top ten in stolen bases, the All-Star game in '81, or that in 1980 he held the National League batting title with an average of .324. No, they will only remember that defining moment when that ground ball went between his legs, to the left side of his glove, and rolled into the grassy field behind him.

That is just so like us petty and trifling human beings. Always remembering the worst possible things and pushing those good attributes and qualities to the back of the book in our minds and sometimes completely off the page and out of memory. But believe me, it is nothing new. It's been going on for years.

Two thousand years ago, the hand-picked disciple named Thomas suffered a similar fate in his loyalty to none other than Jesus himself. Thomas was an in-your-face kind of believer and supporter. He was fearless and often the first one to step up and declare his allegiance. When Jesus got the call Lazarus had died, some of the Twelve advised him not to go back to Bethany. They said, "They'll try to kill you!" But when Jesus held firm that he was going, it was a brave Thomas who said to the others:

Let us go also that we may die with him.

—John 11:16

When Jesus told his disciples, "You know the way to the place where I am going," it was Thomas who had the courage and the mettle to speak up and say to Jesus:

Lord, we don't know where you are going, so how can we know the way.

—John 14:5

And there are more incidents you can look up that will tell you about Thomas's true heart. But the only thing we tend to remember about him is when he doubted for one brief second. He, unlike the other ten disciples, had not seen the resurrected Jesus on Easter night, so he spoke his mind to his friends and said:

Unless I see the nail marks in his hands and put my finger where the nails were, and put my hand into his side, I will not believe it.

—John 29:25

Turned out none of the Eleven believed the truth of the Resurrection until they saw for themselves with their own eyes. Thomas just happened to be the one honest enough to express it. And "doubting Thomas" has become a part of our language for all these years. Jus' taint fair, is it, Thomas? Is it, Bill?

So be careful out there. And remember, everyone you meet has a camera and a video recorder in their pocket today just waiting to catch your one defining moment for everyone to remember.

Books

I love books! Wow, that's a severe understatement. We have books in every room of the house. Shelved and in order. Some stacks are what we read last. Other stacks are what we plan to read next. One room is full of just research books that have become somewhat dated with the arrival and development of the internet. Getting rid of some of those well-worn and oft-used tomes was one of the harder things I've ever done. Years ago, as the computer was becoming more a part of my life, I realized those couple of sets of encyclopedias in the den were just taking up space. I called libraries, schools, charities, friends, enemies—just anyone who would answer the phone—but no one wanted two twenty-six-volume sets of outdated fun, facts, and history. I had to junk them and I felt guilty for months.

In 1982, when The Statlers bought our old grade school and turned it into our home offices and headquarters, the school library was stocked and intact with books, some that had been there when I attended as an elementary student. I asked that no one touch the room as I wanted to see to it myself. I mentioned to my mother what I planned to do, and she enthusiastically said, "I want to go, too."

So, every night for a week, she and I went over to the old school, now our office complex, after hours and took every individual book off its shelf, wiped it clean of dust, washed the shelves, and replaced them in our own decided order and time. She loved it as much as I did. We talked and laughed and remembered reading this and that book as different generational kids. I told her I could smell the pages of an old book and tell if it was any good or not. She thought that was funny and decided to try it; but every time she did, she'd go into a sneezing fit. The memories I have of those few precious nights get sweeter with each passing year. Just Mom and me and a roomful of books.

Old books are fun but they can be downright serious. Remember Josiah in the Bible? Because of the death of his father, he became King of Judah when he was eight years old. Yes, you read that right. He was eight years old! This was around 640 B.C., but I'm sure the folks even back then found it a little unusual to have a monarch on the throne who had yet to learn his multiplication tables and all the state capitals. But Jo persevered, and at the age of twenty-six, hit his stride.

The temple in Jerusalem was in ruins, and the king gave orders for its renovation. In doing so, workers found some dusty old scrolls called the Book of Law. (We are pretty sure it was our book of Deuteronomy that had been lost for ages.) He was so moved in discovering this forgotten treasure that he called all the people together, along with the priests and prophets, and read aloud this entire book to them. The finding and public reading of these sacred pages began a new, reformed era like Judah had never seen. Josiah began cleaning up Dodge. He purged the temple of all cult objects and heathen altars that had gathered there through the years. Platforms used in worshipping the sun, the moon, and the stars were ripped out, smashed to pieces, and burned.

Idolatrous priests were executed, and the Feast of the Passover, long ignored, was reinstated and celebrated. Young Josiah cleaned house for the Lord. And it all took place because someone found some old pages covered with the dust of time that carried a message from God.

Of course, when we remember him, we say, "Josiah? Isn't that the boy king who was only eight years old?" When we should remember him the way the Scriptures do:

> *He did what was right in the eyes of the Lord and walked in all the ways of his father David, not turning aside to the right or to the left.*
>
> —2 Kings 22:2

I have many of Mom's books on my shelves, but the best one is on a table in our living room. It's her leather-bound Bible with her name engraved on it. Inside are still the items she kept there and added to all through the years. Family marriage announcements, obituaries, newspaper clippings of school events, baptismal programs, a few special pictures, a letter or two. Personal memories between the pages of Scriptures. I love picking it up, touching it, and leafing through it every so often. It reminds me of those nights she and I rearranged the old school library. It's like a visit. And sometimes, that's more than the old heart can handle.

Who Are You?

Who are you?

The answer to that question may change from day to day. Certainly, from time to time. I would imagine many of us have been asked to write a reference for someone seeking a new job or an entrance into a club. It's usually a friend or relative or business associate who gives your name to that potential employer or that board of regents who will decide if the applicant is of good enough character to hobnob with those already firmly implanted in the desired organization. And I will go further in saying you have probably found yourself staring at a blank sheet of paper, trying to figure out the best way to present and sell this person. Where do you start? You want to describe them honestly and impressively. You want to embellish their good points and skip over their bad ones. And you want to do all this in a way that won't reflect back on you should they prove to be less than you say they are. You don't want to lose your integrity in marketing this person as best you can, and yet you don't want to let them down by telling the world the absolute truth about them. So, before this reference-writing is all over, it becomes more about who *you* are than who *they* are.

The best preparation for such a duty, is to sit down sometime and write a letter of recommendation for yourself.

Look at yourself honestly and openly and see if you can tell the world just exactly who you are from the inside out. What defines you? What makes you think as you do? What determines the decisions you make, the mistakes you have made? What was truly behind your greatest accomplishment? How truthfully responsible were you for your worst failure? This could painfully become the most difficult and important letter you've ever written.

I am saddened today when I read and observe the way people view the world around them. Politics has become the absolute first consideration. It is how we are seen and judged on the spot, and, actually, nothing else matters after that. We're skewered and cooked on whatever party leanings show through the curtain we all live behind. And quite frankly, I refuse to be defined by that. That is not the most important thing in my life, and it shouldn't be in anyone else's.

How about we look at someone's heart as a first view? Do they have any faith at all, or do they depend on their own wiles and ways to get them through life? Do they trust in a belief they see as bigger than themselves? Are they kind? Considerate? Fair-minded? Trustworthy? Are they self-centered, or do they show empathy for those around them who are less fortunate and less privileged? These are the things that are important.

The pre-Apostle Paul comes strangely to mind right about here, and it makes me smile sadly to think about him. What if Paul had come to you or me and asked us to write a letter on his behalf because he wanted to join our church, or join a social club we are members of, or maybe even want a job with the company we work for. Does what we know about him make us squirm and try to get out of the obligation, or do we man up and write the truth? Do we write what he wants us to, or do we write what we feel and know about him? And just exactly what do we know about him? Well, here is a thumbnail sketch of him in his own words:

> *I am a Jew, born in Tarsus of Cilicia, but brought up in this city. Under Gamaliel I was thoroughly trained in the law of our fathers and just as zealous for God as any of you are today. I persecuted the followers of this Way to their death, arresting both men and women, and throwing them into prison, as also the high priest and all the Council can testify. I even obtained letters from them to their brothers in Damascus and went there to bring these people as prisoners to Jerusalem to be punished.*
>
> —Acts 22:3–5

He punished, threw into prison, and killed people because they believed in Jesus? Thank you, Paul, old pal, but I think I'll pass on writing that letter telling the world what a great guy you are. No hard feelings, understand, but I really don't want to go on record endorsing a man with your background. I'm sorry, but I'm just not putting my neck out that far.

But God did. And maybe the greatest Christian who ever lived was given a second chance. Without Paul, the New Testament would be a thin book. Without Paul, the Word may never have gotten to the Gentiles (that would be me and possibly you). We don't have the ability to see and change the true character of a person as God does, but we do have the capability of using the instincts and compassion he has provided us with to extend mercy and kindness to those who need it.

Every day we change and grow and become a better version of who we are. And so does that next-door neighbor you find so annoying. Go easy on him.

Saying Grace

There is an old story that has been bouncing around our family for years that came to mind recently. You know the kind I'm talking about. Every family has them, and they come up whenever everyone gets together for holidays. This one has been told so often in my family that I don't know now for sure if I actually remember it or if I've heard it so often I only *think* I remember it. "They" say that when I was about five years old, we were invited to my great-uncle's house for dinner. (I honestly have no recollection of the man at all.) As we all sat down to the table, he started passing the food, and I said, "Is nobody going to say the blessing?" Everyone, I'm told, laughed, and he asked me to say the blessing. I did, and a lifelong folk tale was added to the family stack of stories.

Now the only thing I would add to all this is that it sounds like I was a little smart-aleck brat who spoke up when he probably *shouldn't* have and got by with more than he *should* have. But I guess the point was made, and Great-Uncle Caleb (or whatever his name was) must have been a pretty decent guy for taking it so well. What I like to glean from this tale is that it was always a family tradition to say grace at every meal at our house from as far back as I remember. I recall that we would always take turns and take pride when it was our time to offer thanks for the food before us.

The Bible is very clear on giving thanks. Matthew 15 tells the story of Jesus feeding the four thousand with seven loaves of bread: *He told the crowd to sit down on the ground. When he had taken the seven loaves and given **thanks**, he broke them and gave them to the disciples, and they in turn to the people.*

Matthew 14 tells the story of feeding the five thousand with five loaves and two fish: *Taking the five loaves and two fish and looking up to heaven, he gave **thanks** and broke the loaves.*

And then Matthew 26 paints the beautiful picture of the Lord's Last Supper: *While they were eating, Jesus took bread, gave **thanks** and broke it and gave it to his disciples.*

Each time in these verses, Jesus teaches us to give thanks for our daily bread. And not just one day a year but *every* day. Three times a day. At every meal. Daniel 6 tells us he got down on his knees and prayed three times a day. Acts 27:35 tells us Paul *took some bread and gave thanks to God.* If it's good enough for Paul and Daniel, it's good enough for you and me.

A survey was published not long ago that stated 44 percent of Americans say grace before each meal. I was shocked and pleased. I didn't think it would be that high.

It went on to say that 50 percent say grace at their Thanksgiving meal. I was shocked again. I was hoping it would be much, much higher.

So, this tells me there is one thing we all didn't have for Thanksgiving, and that is prayer. But I hope everyone had the sweetest and most peaceful and most restful day of the year. And I hope that as this Thanksgiving season ends and the Christmas season begins, all of God's good blessings will be with each of you and all your families.

P.S.
A perfect conclusion for that family story would be that Great-Uncle Caleb (?) said a table grace for every meal thereafter for the rest of his life. But I don't know that that happened. It would make a great Hollywood ending though, wouldn't it?

Yom Kippur

Early on in our musical career, The Statlers toured extensively with the *Johnny Cash Show*. It was the largest touring troupe in country music at the time, and I began this journey in my life at the young age of eighteen. For the first couple of years, there was a company that would join us in major cities that handled all the merchandise and the selling of program books to the audience at each performance. A Jewish man by the name of Abie was an employee. He was a small, older man who had a winning personality and a sharp sense of humor that kept us entertained constantly backstage. From day one, Abie mistook me as a fellow Jew, even though we sang gospel songs on the show every night. He always singled me out and confided, with little asides, things of his Jewish culture that he thought no one else understood but me. What Abie never caught was that I was as in the dark as everyone else in earshot. But maybe it was his treatment of me that got me interested in the Jewish beliefs and history that so fascinate me to this day.

There is a famous quote by President Harry Turman I have always been drawn to:

> *There is nothing new in the world except the history you do not know.*

So, thanks to little Abie and to Harry, I have had a growing interest in the Jewish way of life most of my existence.

The Old Testament and the Jewish faith are the historical foundations of our Bible. Jesus was of this faith, as were God's chosen people, and that, I feel, is reason enough to be a little versed in their beliefs and rituals. Their Yom Kippur begins on a Sunday in September at sunset and runs through Monday until nightfall. It's a total of twenty-five hours. The meaning of these two strange sounding words is "Day of Atonement," and it comes every year on the tenth day of the seventh month in the Jewish calendar. It's the holiest day of their year, and a day of intense prayer, fasting, and calling out to God for mercy and grace. Here are five interesting things all Jews abstain from on Yom Kippur.

1. Eating and drinking
2. Wearing of leather shoes
3. Bathing or washing
4. Perfumes or lotions
5. Marital relations

They pray for forgiveness and that their name will be entered into God's book of life for the coming year. Then they are obliged to make amends to any other human beings whom they might have offended or sinned against. It can be a very painful, stressful, uncomfortable, and yet religious day for every suffering Jewish believer. And where does all this come from? From our Bible. I refer us all to the book of Leviticus 16:29–30.

This is to be a lasting ordinance for you: On the tenth day of the seventh month you must deny yourselves and not do any work—whether native-born or an alien among you—because on this day atonement will be made for you, to cleanse you. Then, before the Lord, you will be clean from all your sins. It is a sabbath of rest and you must deny yourselves; it is a lasting ordinance.

And there it is. The Jewish law in our Scriptures for all to see. Reading and being understanding of these customs and laws, which are still followed by these good people, can be very eye-opening for us. And yet it can be very confusing to those who believe so differently.

We can respect Jewish laws and holy days and at the same time be so very thankful for our Christian belief in Jesus, the Son of God. All the laws in the world won't get us closer to heaven because we have the Cross. We don't have days of fasting for atonement. We have the Blood. And we can celebrate that all year long. We can give thanks and give glory for the salvation and the grace that was given through one act of suffering that took the place of all the pain of *human* suffering so many go through. Just believe and it is ours. Isn't that just the most beautiful thought in the entire world? Nothing for us to do. Nothing for us to lose. Nothing for us to suffer. All we have to do is believe and heaven is ours!

To our Jewish friends, believers in the one God, we offer good wishes on their holy day.

The Sabbath and the Lord's Day

It is no secret that the Sabbath and the Lord's Day are two completely different things. Some may call our Sundays the Sabbath, but this just isn't the case. The Sabbath is spelled out clearly in the Old Testament. One good example is:

> *Remember the Sabbath day by keeping it holy. Six days you shall labor and do all your work, but the seventh day is a sabbath to the Lord your God.*
> —Exodus 20:8–10

It is also known as the fourth commandment. The Sabbath was, is, and always will be Saturday. From sundown Friday till sundown Saturday. It is as it was meant to be. The commandment goes on to say no working. The Lord made the world in six days, and then he rested on the seventh and you should, too. He made it holy and you should respect and honor that.

Then along comes we New Testament Christians, living under grace instead of the law, and our allegiance goes to the *first* day of the week.

Early on the first day of the week, while it was still dark, Mary Magdalene went to the tomb and saw that the stone had been removed from the entrance.

—John 20:1

Resurrection Day became the Protestant day to keep holy. The day to worship and honor the risen Jesus. The day to rest and not work.

Thus, another story from the Reid family files of memories to emphasize a point. Brother Harold, sister Faye, and I took turns keeping our widowed and much-loved mother occupied and entertained the last six years of her life. We were honored to do so and often vied for the opportunity to do it. She was with one of us and our families almost every day even though she continued to live alone. It was for a summer Sunday-afternoon ride the year she turned ninety that Harold and Brenda picked her up and wound up in Charlottesville. During this casual trek across Afton Mountain from Staunton, Mom mentioned she was in need of a new, small rug for her front porch. Without further ado, Harold pulled into Sam's Club and the three of them got out and went inside. Now, the only way to buy my mother something was to take it to her, because if she was with you, there was no way she would let you pay for anything. That was deeply imbedded in her Depression-influenced, pay-as-you-go makeup. So, she found a little rug to her liking, paid for it, and all was well. Sometime on the way back home, she said from the backseat, "Well, that was a first."

"A first what?" Harold asked.

"The first time I have ever bought something on a Sunday."

"What? You've never bought anything on a Sunday?"

"Nope."

"Not even bread and milk?"

"Never."

"Nothing from the drugstore?"

"Not on a Sunday."

Harold came to me that week and confessed he felt terrible about what had happened and about the role he had played in it. I assured him Mom wasn't upset about it and neither should he be, and that it was just one of those things none of us were aware of. But the next time all the families got together, I made a point to say out loud, "Can you believe that my brother made our ninety-year-old mother break a sacred tradition of hers and buy a rug on a *Sunday*? What a horrible thing that was to do!" (I had to do this to him because he would have done it to me.)

We all laughed about it and have many times since, and no one more than Mom. But I've often thought, ninety years? That's a lifetime commitment. A rare loyalty to a belief. A strong sense of strict values in keeping the Lord's Day separate and holy. I don't think we'll ever see the likes of her again. She was harder on herself than she ever was on any of us.

She is clothed with strength and dignity; she can laugh at the days to come. She speaks with wisdom, and faithful instruction is on her tongue. She watches over the affairs of her household and does not eat the bread of idleness. Her children arise and call her blessed.

—Proverbs 31:25–28

The Man in Charge

Peter and the other disciples watched Jesus ascend into heaven. Rise into the clouds and disappear. This all took place on the Mount of Olives, sometimes called Mount Olivet. Luke tells us in the book of Acts it was a hill a Sabbath's day walk from Jerusalem. (Jews were forbidden to walk very far on the Sabbath, and the measure is considered to be about a half mile.)

The Eleven returned to the upper room, and being the good historian he was, Luke named each disciple present: Peter, John, James, Andrew, Philip, Thomas, Bartholomew, Matthew, James the son of Alphaeus, Simon the Zealot, and Judas son of James. (Judas Iscariot was dead.) There were women there, including Mary the mother of Jesus and also Jesus' brothers.

A gathering of about 120 believers was assembled when we see the first full leadership of Peter after Jesus had left the earth, because it was Simon Peter who stood among the crowd and acclaimed what new business had to be taken care of immediately. He said, "Brothers, the Scripture had to be fulfilled concerning Judas and it is written in the book of Psalms, *'may another take his place of leadership.'* So, we must choose someone to take Judas' place among us."

Peter went on to explain to them that it had to be someone who had been with them from the very beginning, from the time John the Baptist baptized Jesus in the Jordan River until he was taken up into heaven.

> *Therefore it is necessary to choose one of the men who have been with us the whole time the Lord Jesus was living among us, beginning from John's baptism to the time when Jesus was taken up from us. For one of these must become a witness with us of his resurrection.*
> —Acts 1:21–21

There were always other men who traveled and ministered with the Twelve during the three years they learned and preached with Jesus, and two prominent names came up as replacements: Justus and Matthias. They prayed over the matter at Peter's guidance, and then they cast lots (rolled the dice) to see God's will. The lot fell to Matthias and he became the new twelfth disciple.

Earlier, back in the book of Luke, Jesus appointed a larger group of disciples and apostles than just his faithful twelve.

> *After this the Lord appointed seventy-two others and sent them two by two ahead of him to every town and place where he was about to go.*
> —Luke 10:1

These seventy-two men were certainly a part of the 120 believers who were with Peter and the others when the lots were cast. It is a fair assumption that Justus (aka Joseph, as well as Barsabbas) and Matthias were from that group, which explains how they qualified as knowing Jesus from baptism to resurrection. It's interesting to note here that nothing else is ever known about Matthias and he is never mentioned again in the Bible. Even church histories outside the Scriptures disagree on his demise. Some claim he was martyred while others say he died a natural death. The fact is we just don't know any more about him.

But before we leave Peter at this point, it's worthwhile to note that it was Peter alone who set the qualifications of becoming an apostle because nowhere in the Scriptures is it spelled out until his explanation of the procedure. He never shunned the responsibility of taking charge and performing the duties that fell to him. He was a true leader, in service to his Lord to the very end.

QUESTION FOR THOUGHT

What is the difference between a disciple and an apostle?

ANSWER

The quick and easy answer is that a disciple is a pupil or follower while an apostle is someone sent out on a mission. Therefore, an apostle is also a disciple but a disciple is not necessarily an apostle. Peter and Paul, together, later complicated this answer when it was subsequently added that an apostle must have known Jesus personally. And even though Paul was converted after the Ascension, he did meet Jesus on the road to Damascus, thus making him an apostle.

Yeah, I Thought So

Have you ever done something stupid that you felt both sorry for and embarrassed about? Yeah, I thought so. I have a long list of those moments, and every time I get past one, I promise myself it will be my last. But guess what, it never is. I'll just keep at it till I get it right, and in the meantime, I'll continue to be haunted by the words of a great old country song:

When I've learned enough to really live, I'll be old enough to die.

"When I've Learned Enough to Live"
—Buddy Killen, Ray Barker,
Delbert Whitson

Bottom line, living long has nothing to do with it. We're just humans and that's how we bend. We'll never get it right.

I must have been nine or ten years old. It was mid-June, and a friend of mine and I were each on our bicycles, roaming around looking for the perfect summer day. We had stopped at a small grocery store on the main highway for ice cream and a drink. Coming out of the store, each with a Grapette soda in hand, we climbed back on our dusty, old Schwinns and continued on our journey. As we were pulling to the edge of the driveway, something happened so quickly

I hardly knew what it was. Putting on my brakes, I skidded in the gravel, and my front wheel turned into the traffic. A large truck swerved to miss me and I rammed into its side. My bike and I were sprawled into the middle of the road, and there I lay, with cars stopping and people running toward me. The first thing I was aware of, as I saw this rush of concerned folks coming at me, was that I was still holding my Grapette in my right hand. Never spilled a drop. I was lifted up, inspected, and then released by a number of adults who seemed to know what they were looking for. I got back on my bike, a little rattled and confused, and headed for home.

When I got there, I went straight to my room and stretched out on the bed and fell asleep. The next thing I was aware of was my mother sitting on the edge of the bed rubbing my back and waking me. Someone had called her and informed her of what had happened. Her first gentle words to me were, "You need to get up. You should never go to sleep in case you bumped your head. Let's get up and walk around a little."

That was my mother. I was never scolded for being reckless. Never questioned about being careless. She assumed I was smart enough and sensitive enough to learn from my mistakes, and her only concern was for my welfare. And isn't that just exactly like God and how he treats us? He doesn't scold us for every mistake we make. He doesn't punish us every time we do a foolish thing. No matter how many times we may do it, he tends to let us learn on our own and gives us the opportunity to correct it. That's called forgiveness, the love of God, and good parenting.

My stronghold of faith is David. He got tripped up and tripped himself up as many times as any of us have, and he learned something from each senseless episode. There were better people in the Bible than David, but there were none with a more faithful heart and sense of right and wrong. Reading his stories, we marvel at how God could forgive him for all the trouble he seemed to cause for himself. But then, read his Psalms and we see the misery and the pain his very soul was in, and we realize if David was a man of faith, we can be, too.

> *Search me, O God, and know my heart*
> *Try me, and know my thoughts*
> *And see if there be any wicked way in me*
> *And lead me in the way everlasting*
> —Psalm 139:23–24

Right along here I would quote from another country song if there were one that could come anywhere close to the depth-of-heart feelings that just seemed to flow out of King David.

Those senseless and careless episodes didn't stop when I was ten years old. I carried them right on through to the adult years and added to their number with hardly any effort at all. And I'd be ashamed to admit that here if I thought that you hadn't done the same. You have, haven't you? Yeah, I thought so.

Christmas in America

We have all seen it happen in our lifetimes. The religious side of Christmas gets inched over a little more each year. Nativity scenes are outlawed on public-owned grounds. Say "Happy Holidays" instead of "Merry Christmas." Schools have winter break now instead of Christmas break. And we ask ourselves what we can do about it. But first we have to ask ourselves how we got to where we are today.

To begin with, the Christmas season was originally supposed to begin on Christmas Day and end twelve days later on Epiphany. That would be January 6th, the day accepted by the church as representing when the wise men arrived to visit the house where Jesus, Mary, and Joseph were staying. Thus, the Twelve Days of Christmas. But we have gotten way off course from that. Now, our Christmas season starts somewhere in October and *ends* on Christmas Day. Completely backward from how it was meant to be. And why? That's an easy one. Shopping! Commerce! There's no other answer. We've done it to ourselves.

Christmas was basically just a family and community celebration until the mid-1860s in America. It all began to change in 1867 when Macy's department store stayed open until midnight on Christmas Eve. We were never the same. Think about that for a moment. Just two years after the Civil

War, and this huge retail store remained open until the midnight hour so people could shop right up till Christmas morning. Seven years later, in 1874, Macy's put up their first window display with a full Christmas theme. There was no stopping us now.

In 1920, Gimbel's in Philadelphia organized and presented the first Thanksgiving Day parade. And guess who brought up the end of that glorious procession? You're right, Santa Claus himself. No clearer statement could be made that as soon as Thanksgiving was over, Christmas began. Hudson's department store in Detroit and Macy's in New York followed suit with their own parades. Let the shopping season commence!

During World War II in the early 1940s, Americans were prompted to mail Christmas cards and gifts early so service men and women overseas would get them on time. This also set a precedent for an earlier and longer shopping period that we never recovered from. We just went with the flow, and the whole country was Christmas shopping in November.

Abraham Lincoln established a day of thanksgiving in 1863. For the next seventy-six years we celebrated this thoughtful and peaceful day on the fourth Thursday of November. But come 1939, Franklin Roosevelt moved that back to the third Thursday in November to give folks more time to shop between the two holidays. An extra week to commercialize it all. Two years later, it was moved back to the fourth Thursday, but the message had been sent. Get out there and shop and take advantage of those Santa sales!

So how did Christmas get so secular? Not much mystery there, really. We did it and we keep doing it. We yell a little bit every year about the atheists and how they're trying to take Jesus completely out of the picture. But it isn't all their fault. There are things we can do on a personal basis that would keep Christ in Christmas and set an example for all who might care.

1. Read a few verses from the Christmas story in the Bible with the family each evening and then talk about it.

2. When you shop for the less fortunate, take the kids or grandkids with you. It might be catching for them to see what you do.

3. Go to church. Get involved in some duty you've never done before.

4. Go caroling. Learn the third and fourth verses to some of those carols you love.

5. Spread the joy! Smile at everybody you see.

6. Surprise someone with a short visit.

7. Drive down your main street through the heart of town at dusk and look at the Christmas lights as they're coming on. They look golden just before dark and it'll move you.

8. Buy a little, simple, inexpensive gift for someone you've never bought for before. It stretches the heart and brings a smile around the eyes of the person you hand it to.

9. When you feel the stress of the season coming down on you, stop and say a prayer.

10. Every day during Christmas season, do something that makes your heart feel good. You'll find what it is. And if not, it will find you.

Today in the town of David a Savior has been born to you; he is Christ the Lord.

—Luke 2:11

Thus is the Christmas season!

Save Me a Seat

I read a news story a few years ago about saving someone a seat in church in a Midwestern town that quickly turned sour. I won't use any city or even denominational names, but a baby-blessing service was taking place on a Sunday morning, and someone had saved seats up front for family members. A man came in (let's call him Bubba), apparently not family, sat down in one of the seats, and an argument ensued right there in the pews. After the service, it spilled over into the parking lot, and somebody punched somebody in the nose, somebody was run down by a car, and finally the seat-stealer, Bubba, ended up in the county jail on aggravated assault and disorderly conduct. Not the ideal finish you might desire or expect for a Sunday-morning worship service.

This practice of roping off a row or two of seats for special events is not out of the ordinary for most congregations. I've seen it happen many times but have never seen these kinds of results. It is common practice at weddings and funerals, of course, and I can't imagine why anyone would object to it unless there were underlying difficulties in that family situation that we are not privy to. (I'd have to bet the morning collection plate on that!)

No surprise, though, this is not the first family to create and have a little problem over seating arrangements when it comes to our religion. The book of Matthew tells us Salome, the mother of the disciples James and John, came to Jesus one day, knelt in front of him, and said, "I have a favor to ask of you."

"What is it you want?" Jesus asked.

"I would like to ask for two seats in your kingdom. One for each of my sons. One to sit at your right and the other at your left."

Now, Salome has always struck me as being a little pushy where her boys were concerned. I think of her as maybe the first stage mother in history. She wanted to move them to the front of the line, ahead of the other ten disciples, and get special privileges for them by getting them special seating. Scripture tells us the other ten were not happy over this attempted manipulation, and in stark and honest words, Jesus let her and her sons know he wasn't either.

"You don't know what you're asking," Jesus answered. "These places belong to those for whom my Father has prepared."

I can't imagine how Salome, a devotee, so much in the inner circle that she was one of the women at the tomb on Easter morning with Mary Magdalene, felt after being turned down by Jesus. Nor how James and John must have coped with it when it was all over. And all because, just like in that little church out West, someone wanted to save someone a seat.

The one time I know it *was* successful was back about 1,500 years before this Salome incident ever happened. There is no mention of any favored or reserved seats in the temples of old, but in the portable tabernacle that the Israelites carried with them in the desert for forty years, there is. In this structure, the Ark of the Covenant, in all its glory, was kept. By instructions from the Lord himself to Moses, this sacred ark was built, completely gilded in gold, and carried from place to place by staves of acacia wood, also gilded, so that it would not be touched by human hands. Atop this unique and hallowed chest was designed a "mercy seat." This seat was reserved only for God, who would sit there and dispense his mercy when blood sacrifices were offered.

As sorry as I am for Bubba sitting in that lonely county jail, it's a lesson for the learning when it comes to saving someone a seat. Even Jesus didn't feel he had the authority to make that promise, and in all the Bible, only God reserved a seat where no one else could sit. As for me, I'll take my chances in a distant pew somewhere toward the back of the church in case another fight breaks out.

> *From ev'ry stormy wind that blows,*
> *From ev'ry swelling tide of woes,*
> *There is a calm—a sure retreat—*
> *Our refuge is the Mercy-seat.*
>   From the poem "The Mercy Seat"
>   —Anonymous

Truth in Songwriting

I've been writing songs since I was about eleven years old. I remember the first one clearly, but please don't ever ask me to sing it for you. It wasn't all that good and most of it I'd rather forget. Make that all of it I'd rather forget. But from that time on, the knack of putting together a song—music and lyric—became an obsession with me. I've been blessed to have hundreds recorded, and by some really fine singers. A good singer can often make a mediocre song sound like a masterpiece. In return, a good song can also make a run-of-the-mill singer sound like he knows what he's doing.

I've been honored to know some of the really good contemporary writers during our career and a few who stand out as geniuses. One would have to be friend and fellow busker Kris Kristofferson. Kris came to Nashville in the mid-sixties and took a job as a custodian at Columbia Studios, where we recorded. We first got to know him there and followed his climb as he started to get a few of his songs recorded. It's no secret he brought something to the art that no one before had brought. He gave his songs an intimacy and a sensitivity that other songsmiths had just never been able to capture. His weren't just clever little short stories, they were novels of emotion that just burst on the paper and the record and the radio.

America fell in love with his stories of romance and feelings, and it wasn't long before they discovered he had more
dimension to his talent than first noted. Being a Rhodes
Scholar and a man who drew heavily on his own insights and
beliefs, Kris wrote a gospel song that took the nation by
storm. "Why Me?" was an attestation to his faith and his
Christianity that had previously not been evident. (In time,
the song would become known as "Why Me, Lord?" and no
one really knows why.)

Remember the Nancy Kerrigan saga? She was the young
Olympic figure skater who was attacked at Cobo Arena in
Detroit in 1994 by the henchmen of her rival. One clubbed
her leg with a police baton to keep her out of the upcoming
competition. That horrible and famous newsclip of her lying
there in pain crying "Why? Why? Why me?" is a hard one
to shake from our memories. But her plea is one that rings
in many of our ears so dramatically, because haven't we all
said, or at least thought sometime in our lives, when something discouraging happened to us, "Why me?" Thus the
brilliance of this country/gospel song. The "why me" is ut-
tered not in alarm but in amazement.

Why me, Lord? What have I ever done
To deserve even one
Of the pleasures I've known
Tell me, Lord, what did I ever do
That was worth loving you
For the kindness you've shown

These words do a complete reverse on what that phrase
usually means. It's powerful and it's theological and it's

scripturally correct. If John Calvin had ever written a song, this would have been it. But listen, there's more.

Lord, help me, Jesus, I've wasted it so
Help me, Jesus, I know what I am
But now that I know that I needed you so
Help me, Jesus, my soul's in your hand

Jesus answered, no one can come to me unless the Father
who sent me draws him.... Everyone who listens to the
Father and learns from him comes to me.
—John 6:44–45

It's surprising all the truth we can learn by just keeping our ears open. And it's surprising from where that truth often comes.

The Witch of Endor

Halloween is upon us. And before that full moon of autumn sets on the last day of this month, the ghosts and hobgoblins will be at our doors. So, how about a story with a little horror and raising of the dead and some scary stuff that makes us jump and scramble and flip on the lights? Okay, let's do it. Let's turn to the book of 1 Samuel and see what we can conjure up that will "shiver me timbers"!

The prophet Samuel was a godly man and a kingmaker. He reluctantly made Saul the first king of Israel. Then Saul lost favor with God and Samuel alike, and when Samuel died, Saul was left with no spiritual counselor to lean on. When the Philistine army, sensing a weakness, came after Saul and lined up for battle, the Scriptures clearly tell us *he was afraid; terror filled his heart* (1 Sam. 28:5). The king badly needed to talk to Samuel for guidance. But how could he do that? Samuel was dead and Saul had outlawed all mediums and sorcerers and witches and warlocks who were purported to be able to communicate with those who had passed to another world.

First, he prayed to God, but God refused to answer him. His next move was to call in his attendants and demand they find him *a woman who is a medium* (1 Sam. 28:7). "There's one over in Endor," they told him.

So, Saul put on other clothes and disguised himself (much like you and I have done on Halloween nights as kids to hide our identity). He waited till dark and took two men with him to the home of this woman and told her to call up a spirit for him. He said, "I'll tell you his name."

But the woman refused to even consider it. Not recognizing him, she said, "Saul has outlawed all spiritualists and seers and if I get caught doing this, it will be the death of me." But Saul insisted and swore to her she would not be punished. The woman, though scared for her life, finally said, "Okay, whom shall I bring up for you?"

Saul looked her in the eye and said simply, "Bring up Samuel," and the woman began her ritual.

When the witch saw Samuel, she cried out at the top of her voice, "Why have you deceived me? You are Saul!"

It was as if seeing Samuel coming up from the grave also revealed Saul's identity to her. The king exclaimed, "Don't be afraid. What do you see?"

The woman, frightened and trembling, said, "I see a spirit coming up out of the ground."

Saul, feeling the tenseness of the moment, demanded, "What does he look like?" The witchy woman said, "An old man wearing a robe is coming up!"

At this moment, Saul knew for sure this was Samuel back from the dead. He fell on the ground and lay face down, surely out of a mixture of respect and fear and shame. Samuel was the next to speak. He asked, "Why have you disturbed me?"

Saul's words came fast and furious, telling Samuel the Philistines were coming after him and God had turned his back on him and that now Saul desperately needed Samuel to tell him what to do.

"Why do you consult me now that the Lord has turned away from you and become your enemy?" Samuel asked. "The Lord has torn the kingdom from your hands because you did not obey him. He will hand over both Israel and you to the Philistines. And tomorrow, you and your sons will be with me."

And it all came true. Just like Samuel said it would from the grave.

This is actually a horrible story of a lost man and a lost nation. The nation would come back to God but the man never would. He would die the next day with his three sons. They in battle, he by his own sword. The Philistines would then behead Saul and hang his body on the wall of their temple.

And the Lord was grieved that he had made Saul king over Israel

—1 Samuel 15:35

This Old Testament tale is interesting yet very scary. And we may even wonder what we should learn from it. The Bible tells us Saul cut an impressive figure and was physically a man without equal among his people. He was the most handsome in all Israel and stood a head taller than all the rest. And when the nation wanted a king, they wanted this striking, charismatic character to lead them. But in simple terms, big, attractive King Saul just got too big for his armor. I think obedience, respect, and a constant love of God is the message we're left with.

If we can remember what Saul forgot, we will remain in the good graces of the Lord.

King Uzziah

When the kingdom split, circa 900 B.C. in Israel, Judah had its own king. For the next four hundred years, they had twenty kings; some good ones, some bad ones. Let's talk about one of the good guys. Of course, even the good ones had their problems, and I think we're going to find Uzziah's story pretty fascinating.

The first thing we need to know about him is that he went by two different names. The book of 2 Chronicles calls him Uzziah; the book of 2 Kings calls him Azariah. But it was all the same fellow. His father before him, Amaziah, got himself assassinated, and Uzziah became king at the age of sixteen. Now, let's pause right here and think for a minute what you and I were doing when we were sixteen years old. As for me, along about that time, I was trying to scrounge up enough money to buy fender skirts for a well-used '55 Chevy and trying to get a date for the prom. Uzziah, on the other hand, was the king of Judah. (Here is where you chime in with what you were doing.)

Uzziah reigned for fifty-two years. Now, that is a pretty good term for anyone in public service, and he had a record that was hard to match. Uzziah was God-fearing and his administration accomplished so much he never had to embellish his record to impress anyone.

- He went to war against the Philistines and won.
- He made peace treaties with many surrounding nations.
- He rebuilt towns all over his region.
- He built towers in the desert and dug cisterns for outlying livestock.
- He put people to work in vineyards and agriculture.
- He built up the army to more than three hundred thousand troops.

Uzziah was a good and progressive monarch and was noted to be one of the outstanding kings in the history of Judah.

And as long as he sought the Lord, God gave him success.

—2 Chronicles 26:5

And then it happened. Something we might think was small but which was not in the eyes of God. The king, for some reason or another, we're never told, decided one day he wanted to burn some incense on the "altar of incense" in the temple. I mean, what harm could that be? Certainly not a sin. But it was. It was in defiance of God. Priests and only priests could perform the burning of incense. This had been handed down from the Law of Moses and had been good enough for everyone for centuries. So, King Uzziah, walking into the temple with fire in his hand, did not go down well at all, no matter how big a man he thought he was.

When he went in to begin this ritual, eighty-one priests— that's eighty-one—converged on him and said, "Whoa, there, King. This is not your job. This is our duty, and one we've been consecrated to do. Leave the sanctuary now! You are being un-faithful by doing this, and you will not be honored by God for your actions."

Well, now a situation was at hand. The king of the land had just been severely reprimanded by a gaggle of priests, and he was insulted, embarrassed, and angered at their insolence. Here stands Uzziah with the flame in his hand, like your grand-daddy getting ready to light his pipe, with the match slowly burning down while he himself simmered and burned. He raged in indignation at the priests as they all stood there in front of the altar of incense. And right in mid-rage, at the height of his fury, little beads of something began popping out on his forehead. The priests immediately recognized it as leprosy, and they grabbed him and ushered him out of the temple away from the people.

God had afflicted him, and King Uzziah had leprosy for the rest of his life until the day he died. He lived in a separate house from his family and was never allowed back into the tem-ple. This was his punishment for the sin of pride. Uzziah got to thinking he was the most important and he could do any-thing he wanted without respect for God and his laws. God enables and encourages us with his blessings, but then, like the human beings we are, we tend to take pride in things we have nothing to do with.

God opposes the proud, but gives grace to the humble
—James 4:6

Uzziah's son Jotham took charge of the palace and gov-erned the people for his father until his own reign began at the age of twenty-five. We're told Jotham grew powerful because he walked steadfastly before God. He remained one of the good guys.

In the Shadow Of

We often have an image of the disciples as being single, free to travel, and with no particular home connections. This was not true of Peter. He was married, had a house, and his mother-in-law lived with him and his wife (Matt. 8:14). This often begs the question of the position of the Catholic Church that claims Peter as their first pope yet forbids their priests and popes to marry. Another question often arises as to whether any of the other disciples were married. Paul, who chose not to take a wife, asks the question in 1 Corinthians 9:5:

> Don't we have the right to take a believing wife along with us, as do the other apostles and the Lord's brothers and Cephas?

So that verse alone tells us some of the others were married, as were Jesus' brothers who were a part of his ministry. And, of course, Cephas/Peter, whose mother-in-law took to her bed with a fever and was healed personally by Jesus by simply touching her hand.

Peter was given this power of healing by Christ, and the stories of how he used it are fascinating and amazing. He and John could just place their hands on someone and they would receive the Holy Spirit. This was the authority entrusted to this man, Peter. This one outstanding story from Acts may tell us best about the dominance empowered in Peter.

He and the other apostles created a habit of meeting often with all the believers in Jerusalem in Solomon's Colonnade. This was sometimes called Solomon's Portico or Solomon's Porch, because that is just what it was—a porch that was built on the east side of the temple but with a roof, which gave a little more protection from the weather than the temple courtyards. As the number of believers grew, the crowds on the porch grew. People from the neighboring towns came, and they brought their family and friends who were sick in body and mind so that Peter could touch them and heal them in the name of Jesus. And he did, but it kept him and the others busy from morning till dusk. It finally came to such overcrowding that people brought their loved ones who were ill and laid them in the streets on beds and cots so that Peter's shadow might fall on them as he passed by. His shadow! He didn't need to speak or touch or say a prayer for them. If just his shadow passed over them, they felt the Spirit. And the Bible tells us all who came were healed.

And all who come to Jesus still are. He turns no one away who believes.

The church was just beginning, and this is such a great example that the church is the people, the believers, not the building. We were without a church building for months and months due to the pandemic of 2020. We were, first, unable to gather, then unable to gather indoors, but we still had a church. We still had a minister and a church family staying in touch through prayer and faith and God-given technology. Our building was empty but our church thrived. Thanks be to God.

QUESTION FOR THOUGHT

Where did Paul go to be schooled and taught personally by Jesus?

ANSWER

Arabia. Paul tells us very clearly in Galatians, first chapter, that he received his teachings from no man, but from Jesus himself. He apparently was there, with revelations from Christ, for three years before he ever went to meet any of the twelve disciples. He is so emphatic about this that he says, "I assure you before God that what I am writing to you is no lie." Then he tells us he went to Jerusalem and met and stayed with Peter for fifteen days.

Cast of Characters

We all know a story is only as good as its cast. The perfect cast is what helps move a good story along, and when God came up with the idea that he wanted to come to earth as a human to get our attention and fulfill his promise, he had to come up with an effective cast of characters to pull it off.

Now, any good play, book, or movie needs a romantic lead, so let's start with the girl. We need a young girl. Some say a teenager, although the Bible doesn't support that, but it does tell us she was a virgin. From this, we will have to leave it up to the individual reader as to her age. She was young and, I believe, pretty, and we'll call her Mary. A beautiful, simple, and lovely name. Mary will give birth to a son. Yes, a Virgin Birth. What could be more miraculous and attention-getting than that? Only one thing could be as impossible as a virgin giving birth, and that would be someone coming back from the dead. (But then I get ahead of myself.)

Now, we need a male lead opposite her. Someone strong and in charge, so let's make him a little older to stress his authority. Quite a bit older, by some people's beliefs, although the Bible doesn't support that either. And let's not just make him the romantic lead, let's also make him a man's man. Someone both men and women would like and respect. Let's make him an Everyman. Not a rich man. Not spoiled with the easy life. Make him a farmer or a herdsman or how about a carpenter? That shows he's physically strong and has a skill and intelligence. He's not a ditch digger but someone who uses his hands and his mind and his talent every day. And we'll give him a good, solid, common name that everyone knows. We'll call him Joseph. A man of few words. (And note here that nowhere in the Scriptures does Joseph ever speak a word.)

Now we need a little mystery. A little intrigue. Maybe something supernatural even. That always brings them in and wakes up an audience. How about an angel that comes and talks to the young woman without the man knowing it? And that will fall right in line with the next thing any good story needs...conflict! The angel will provide that, also. He tells the wife-to-be about the birth, she becomes "with child" through the Holy Spirit, the husband-to-be finds out, thinks the worst, and sets out to get rid of his fiancée. Oh, this is getting good now. This could be one of those books you just can't put down or a movie that everyone will want to see.

Then the angel has to come back in the scene by appearing in a dream to the husband-to-be to explain the situation and finally settle the problem. All is now well with Mary and Joseph on the same side and ready to face the world.

A baby born at home is commonplace. It happens every day, or used to. Maybe born down the street at the doctor's office or the hospital. But that's so humdrum. I mean, where's the drama in that? We have to have something outstanding happen to make this birth different. We'll have them take a trip and not be able to get a hotel room. That has happened sometime or another to everybody who has ever traveled, and all the world will be able to relate with the frustration and anger and weariness it causes. But all those feelings will double if the wife is not only pregnant but also due. Okay, the inn is full. Where could they be sent? To someone's house? Too easy. Back home? Too far. How about some place so dirty and nasty that no one would ever allow their baby to be born there? No one but almighty God, who wants to make a point. And that point is that the salvation that he is representing is for not just the rich, but also for the poor. So poor and lonely that we'll even have him lying in a manger, a feeding trough for animals, instead of a handmade crib that certainly Joseph cold have whipped up pretty quickly if they had been back at his shop in Nazareth.

Then let's drive that point home about being for all people, the wealthy and the poor and downtrodden. And here's a good way to do it. Let's make the announcement, the first and only announcement of the birth, to a group who is not on the top of the social ladder. Shepherds. They are unskilled laborers and fall into the lower class. So, many of them are ne'er-do-wells and criminal types who go from area to area doing odd jobs. Let's go directly to them with the news and have them be the absolute first ones to visit the newborn baby. And then we will widen the scope and bring in the wealthy and the wise. We'll have them come from far off, showing this salvation will eventually cut a wide swath. They will arrive bringing their rich and expensive gifts, and then we have covered the entire spectrum.

And why not use Herod one more time before he is erased entirely from the picture? A more evil and malevolent king cannot be found than one who kills babies to protect his own station in life. This should make him the most disgusting villain in all history.

This is turning out to be a pretty good story and with a pretty good cast. It just might be one that people will want to see a second and third time; actually read it all the way through again and again. We'll throw in some chanting angels, a mysterious star that moves around in the heavens, messages in people's dreams, and maybe even an exile into Egypt and back. It gives it adventure and suspense. And then there is always that thread of warmth running through it that is the relationship between mother and child. The mother taking everything in, reflecting on it, remembering it, and pondering it in her heart.

After all that is said, what is left to say? We have him born into the world without it being a run-of-the-mill birth. His childhood and adolescence are not really of great import. It's what he's going to do when he becomes a man. Oh, he could start preaching when he's ten or twelve years old, but who's going to listen? He has to be an adult to gain any real respect and notice. So, we'll just skip from his birth, maybe touch on one youthful story, and then go right to his baptism and the beginning of his ministry. That should be good enough and all we need.

And sure enough it *is* all we need. All we need for Christmas. What a story!

> *Who do you think would believe such a thing?*
> *Would believe that this story is true?*
> *Who do you think would believe such a thing?*
> *Well, here's hoping to heaven you do*
> > "Who Do You Think?"
> > —Harold Reid, Don Reid

The Clock

A few years ago, Debbie and I were shopping in Dayton, Virginia, at the Farmers Market. We were casually strolling through all the little stores and came upon one gift shop with a wall full of beautiful and unusual clocks. One caught my fancy immediately. (Caught my fancy—don't think I have ever used that phrase before in my life. Sounds like something my grandmother might have said.) Every hour, the face of this clock would separate into a dozen pieces going every which way and then come back into place. All the time this was happening, instead of chiming, it would play an old hymn. I stood fascinated and asked the clerk to make it happen again. He did, over and over. I had never seen anything like it and was completely charmed by it.

Flash ahead to about two months later, and it's Christmas morning. I opened the package, and Debbie had given me this very clock because of the look on my face when I first saw and heard it. I was in love. The only question left was where to hang it. She took care of that also by placing it on the wall in our family den, right by the chair where I sit most of the time, reading with my dog, Lucy, on my lap. Every day, every hour, I hear it *on* the hour playing a beautiful traditional hymn: about thirty seconds at noon of "What a Friend We Have in Jesus." 1 P.M., "Amazing Grace." 2 P.M.,

"How Great Thou Art." 3 P.M., "In the Garden." 4 P.M., "Jesus Loves Me." Then repeat.

It gives such a peace to me and to the house that I vowed to myself to stop whatever I might be doing and listen to it every time it played. I am still true to that self-promise, and it has been a blessing that I look forward to even after all these years.

I realized one day, while stopping in my tracks and closing my eyes as one of the tunes rang through the rooms, that this is exactly what David had done for Saul. This was my mechanical David.

1 Samuel 16 tells us the spirit of the Lord left King Saul and an evil spirit from God came and tormented him and wouldn't let him have any peace of mind. Some of his attendants saw what was happening and came up with a very early theory on musical therapy. They said to him, "Let us go find someone who might come here to your room and play the harp for you. The music will sooth you and make you feel better."

Saul relented and said, "Find someone who plays well and bring him to me." (I've always smiled at him saying "someone who plays well." Saul didn't want any amateur harp player who didn't know all the notes and all the chords.)

One of the servants offered, "I know a Bethlehemite who can do the job. He's very talented and cunning in his playing. He's the son of Jesse. He's also a warrior. A very brave man. He's handsome and he speaks well. And the Lord is with him."

That's all Saul needed to hear. He sent a message to Jesse and told him to send his son to him. Obediently, Jesse took a donkey, loaded him down with bread, a skin of wine, and a young goat, and sent them with his son David to appease the king. The end result is best told in the words of Samuel himself:

Whenever the spirit from God came upon Saul, David would take his harp and play. Then relief would come to Saul; he would feel better and the evil spirit would leave him.

—1 Samuel 16:23

This little arrangement worked just fine until that day when Saul threw a spear at David right in mid-song and tried to pin him to the wall. Luckily, David was too fast and nimble for the distraught and disturbed king and was able to make good his escape.

I have thrown nothing whatsoever at the clock at any time. It never fails to bring me peace and comfort and remind me hourly just how much old hymns inspire and calm me. And there is another great feature I just love. By touching a little switch on the back, at Christmastime it plays five of my favorite carols.

It ain't David, but it's pretty nice.

Mistakes Were Made

I almost began this sentence with "There was a friend of mine..." But this person was not really a friend of mine. He was just a casual and passing acquaintance whom I really didn't know very well at all. Had he truly been a friend of mine, I probably would know his head and his heart a little better and be able to explain his thought process to you. But I don't and I can't. Here is all I can tell you and it may leave us both a little in the dark.

This man was a professed born-again Christian and was very vocal in what he believed and what he thought everyone else should believe. I, along with many others, heard him say that since he had found God, he no longer sinned.

My reaction to that was, "What?! Then what do you do?"

It's human nature and we can't separate ourselves from sin. Jesus covered us but we're still just humans. We still have to recognize our sins and confess them, but we can't run from them and escape them. Paul knew the struggle when he said:

For what I do is not the good I want to do; no, the evil I do not want to do—this I keep on doing.
—Romans 7:19

Martin Luther gave us more wisdom on this matter of erroneously thinking we become some kind of flawless whitewashed statues of perfection as soon as Jesus enters our picture:

Be a sinner and sin boldly, but behave and rejoice in Christ even more boldly.

Granted, two different times in the Scriptures that I can think of, Jesus forgives and heals someone and says, "Go and sin no more." That happened with the crippled man by the pool at the temple and the woman guilty of adultery. By telling them to go and sin no more, Jesus was telling them not to return to their particular lifestyle of sin. He was telling them to make better choices about the things that had caused them problems. But we have to realize there will be more sin to encounter as none of us are perfect. We're forgiven; but we're not perfect.

For all have sinned and fall short of the glory of God.
—Romans 3:23

Someone recently pointed out to me that outside the pulpit, you seldom hear the word sin. It's not a word you hear on a daily basis. Not in the workplace. Not in school. Not on social media. Not in conversation. It's archaic, outdated, and old-fashioned to say the word "sin." That word immediately makes people feel bad and guilty and belittled. So, what have we done? We've gotten rid of it because we don't want to hurt anyone's feelings and especially don't want to hurt our own. It's been pushed out of our vocabularies by any number of euphemisms that have taken over our language. I'll give you a few examples and then you add some of your own.

character flaw	defect	error in judgment
shortcoming	lapse	slip up
habit	vice	mistake
messed up	my bad	a failing

And the one I despise the most, "mistakes were made." This is the ultimate go-to when no one wants to take responsibility for what they've done. No one wants the wrongdoing laid at their particular feet so they try to lay it at everyone else's in general.

Keep your ears open this week for all the words people will use to keep from saying "sin." We may even be surprised at the words we ourselves use to avoid saying it. Why? Because it's a heavy word. It carries a lot of dark baggage and consequences. You get tempted and you say you slipped up, you made a mistake, you messed up. All of these roll off the tongue so much easier than saying, "I sinned today." Euphemisms make us feel a little less harsh about ourselves and a little less judgmental about others. But the truth of the matter is we sinned today in body, mind, or spirit, and we're going to do it again tomorrow. That's why we have a Savior.

Easter Day

I will get no argument when I say Easter Sunday is the most important day in our Christian calendar. It is our high holy day. A recent survey revealed that the top four church-attendance Sundays of the year are:

1. Easter
2. Christmas
3. Mother's Day
4. Father's Day

It didn't surprise me one bit that poor ole dad was on the bottom of the list. He gets pushed to the back and shuffled to the side whenever a comparative listing of moms and dads show up. But that's okay. All dads will tell you they're just happy to be somewhere on the list.

That same survey revealed that attendance even falls off for the number-three spot—Mother's Day—after the demise of said mother. Isn't it sad that so many folks tend to go to church for family members and actually think that's a good enough reason? And then, when the parents are no longer around, the family slowly drifts away and another pew is glaringly empty and blends in with the other ones up and down the aisle.

The survey goes on to tell us that Christmas attendance is strongly influenced by the simple fact that so many out-of-town families gather and come to church to accommodate the other kin. This can't be a good reason either. Plus, I'm sure we all know there are those out there who call themselves Christians who don't completely believe in the Virgin Birth. (I have even heard of ministers who admit to this and yet still continue their Christmas sermons.)

So, come Easter Sunday, be it sunrise service in the cold morning sun or the regular service in the warmth of the sanctuary, you will see faces you haven't seen in a year. And that's okay, too. Better once-a-year than never-at-all. But even a wayward preacher, here and there, can't say he doesn't believe in the events of this sacred day, because if you don't embrace the Resurrection, there is no way you can rationalize yourself to be called a Christian. This is what the word "Christian" is all about: that you believe, beyond doubt and hesitation, that Jesus arose from the dead because he was the Son of God. And that is my little sermon for the cause and verification of Easter.

Whenever the family travels or vacations together over a weekend, I always have appropriate little quizzes for them for Sunday mornings. I'll share with you a few questions I used to ask the kids when they were small and then again to the grandkids when they came along. You may find them useful in your family. I used these one Easter when our whole gang was away for a family trip.

1. How many people were at the Last Supper?
2. Which disciple told on Jesus?
3. How did this disciple point out Jesus?
4. What color was the robe the soldiers put on Jesus?
5. On what day of the week did Jesus arise?

Then, if you want to engage the adults in your gathering and see what they have absorbed and retained, here are a few harder ones for them. You may send some of them to the Bible for the answers, but that's okay. It does us all well to refresh the facts.

1. What official office did Pontius Pilate hold?
2. Who was the prisoner Pilate released in exchange for Jesus?
3. As Jesus became thirsty on the cross, what was he offered to drink?
4. Whose personal tomb was Jesus taken to?
5. Is the word Easter ever mentioned in the Bible?

Easter is a beautiful and sacred day and one I hope we all can share and feel the closeness of the Holy Spirit. It is the most important day in our faith.

Kids quiz: 1) thirteen; 2) Judas; 3) he kissed him; 4) purple/scarlet; 5) the first

Adult quiz: 1) governor; 2) Barabbas; 3) vinegar; 4) Joseph of Arimathea; 5) once

The stone was rolled away from the door, not to permit Christ to come out, but to enable the disciples to go in.
—Peter Marshall

What Does the Bible Say about It?

How many times a week does that question cross your mind? How many times, when you're trying to come to a solution about an issue, do you wonder if it is addressed in Scripture and in what context? Happens to me all the time. And just when I think I know without looking it up, something tells me I should look it up, and I find out I didn't know after all!

Let's just pull some random topics out of the air that we all probably think are not covered at all in our KJV, or our NIV, our ESV, our NLT, or whatever translation of the OT and NT you have laying on your nightstand or coffee table. Let's start with, I don't know, how about...being lazy. What does the Bible say about it?

> *Go to the ant, O sluggard; consider her ways, and be wise.*
>
> —Proverbs 6:6

> *But if anyone does not provide for his relatives, and especially for members of his household, he has denied the faith and is worse than an unbeliever.*
>
> —1 Timothy 5:8

And there's plenty more where those came from. How about another random subject? Let's say...keeping bad company. What does the Bible say about that?

Do not be deceived: Bad company ruins good morals.
—1 Corinthians 15:33

I do not sit with men of falsehood, nor do I consort with hypocrites.
—Psalm 26:4

This works for almost any topic you can think of. Oh, it might not tell you what you should do if your computer crashes, but it will address everything related to the matter. It covers anger, frustration, anger, disappointment, anger, seeking help, and also anger. And it is never-changing in its advice and comfort. The answers are never altered to fit the times.

- 2 + 2 will always equal 4.
- Ain't is never a valid word.
- The Earth will always revolve around the Sun.
- And the truth will be today what it was yesterday.

We don't expect math and English and science to change, so why do we think the Bible should?

Are there more serious topics and subjects we're faced with today and every day than the ones we've covered here? Of course, there are. There are moral issues and social issues and political issues that storm the gates of our peace and security every single day. Issues that keep us up nights and in turmoil all day long. Sometimes it's not the solutions that trouble us but the execution of those solutions that we know to be truth. It takes courage to face an uncomfortable honesty we try despairingly not to face, or to take a stand when we know it might offend someone we love. It takes commitment to speak the truth when we know we might be vilified and criticized by everyone around us.

> *If the world hates you, know that it has hated me before it hated you.*
> —John 15:18 (words of Jesus)

> *May the grace of the Lord Jesus Christ, and the love of God...be with you all.*
> —2 Corinthians 13:14 (words of Paul)

> *There's a family Bible on the table*
> *Each page is torn and hard to read*
> *But the family Bible on the table*
> *Will ever be my key to memories*
> —"Family Bible" (words of Willie Nelson)

Does God Care Who Wins the Super Bowl?

Super Bowl Sunday! It rolls around every year just like Christmas, Easter, Halloween, your birthday, and the Fourth of July. There is no getting away from it, even if you're not a sports fan. It's in your face on so many different levels, and as frivolous as the question in the title sounds, it isn't bad fodder for thought. And it's certainly a great conversation starter.

Polls and surveys are taken practically every year with similar questions just to test the public on their personal takes as to God's intervention in America's sports obsessions. The Public Religion Research Institute took their survey a few years ago with this question:

Do you believe God determines who wins the Super Bowl?

You may or may not be surprised at this answer, but 27 percent of sports fans gave a resounding "Yes!" That's over a quarter of the folks out there who believe God is in the game. On the other hand, though, that tells us there are 73 percent who believe he's not involved. Legendary Green Bay Packers quarterback Aaron Rodgers has given an interesting personal quote on the matter:

"I don't think God cares a lot about the outcome. He cares about the people involved, but I don't think he's a big football fan."

That same survey asked another question you might find worthy of your mulling:

Have you ever prayed for the outcome of a game?

Twenty-six percent said "Yes," leaving 74 percent asking us to believe they have never said even a small, silent prayer for their favorite team in the last grueling seconds of a one-point game.

And whatever you ask in prayer, you will receive, if you have faith.
—Matthew 21:22

The Super Bowl is the most watched television broadcast in America. Upward of 150 million people will tune in. Some will be watching to see all the new and interesting commercials while others will only be concerned with seeing the over-produced halftime show. Most, however, will be there for the game. Of these total viewers, 26 percent will be praying for their team to prevail and bring home the trophy. That comes out, in round numbers, to be just short of thirty-eight million who will offer up a prayer sometime during the matchup. And if they win, I hope they offer up another one when it's all over, thanking the good Lord for bringing their team through the storm and into the end zone. That is, *if they have faith*. Because everyone who prays for a win is not going to get one. But the beautiful thing about it all is that it may be the only time this week some of those thirty-eight mil will actually be in prayer—the only time they will have that kind of contact with their Maker and really recognize him and speak to him as one they truly can depend upon. Some may even get used to petitioning him again on another matter at hand, and then again, and then again.

> *Do not be anxious about anything, but in everything, by prayer and petition, with thanksgiving, present your requests to God.*
>
> —Philippians 4:6

And before you know it, we might even have them on our team, praying every day, taking their thoughts, their cares, their requests, and their thanks to the Lord, just like Paul suggests in this verse. And who knows, God just may have used the Super Bowl to bring some new people to their knees on a daily basis. Don't put it past him. He's pretty clever in the way he brings his will into every aspect of our lives.

This Super Bowl Sunday, when we're on the sofa eating chips and dip and watching all the activities getting ready to happen, let's be among those thirty-eight million and offer up a prayer for the safety and good will of both sides of the field. And if we happen to have a good time watching, that's okay, too.

And who knows, Aaron, God just might enjoy a good football game after all.

Friday the 13th

Just how superstitious are you? There are degrees, you know. Some people live in excessive fear of crossing the boundaries of black cats and broken mirrors. I have never been one to live in that kind of extreme terror. I would have to say my view of these kinds of things is more cartoonish than serious. Not to say I willingly will walk under a ladder, but the main reason I won't is because I don't want a bucket of paint falling on my head, not because of some witchery that may befall me if I do. I also don't open an umbrella indoors, but that is specifically because it doesn't rain indoors and not because of something horrible that may happen to me should I do such a silly thing. However, I have often wondered just where all of these little annoyances come from and how they have been purported by reasonably intelligent people such as ourselves. And what I discovered was that the dread of a Friday the 13th has a biblical basis. Trust me, I wasn't expecting that.

First, let's get the definition out of the way. According to *Merriam-Webster*, the definition of superstition is:

> 1. a belief or practice resulting from ignorance, fear of the unknown, trust in magic or chance, or a false conception of causation

2. an irrational abject attitude of mind toward the supernatural, nature, or God resulting from superstition

Now, loaded with that information, let's retain all that while we peruse the calendar and discover there are usually one or two Fridays in every year that fall on the thirteenth day of a month. Sometimes three! We are now armed and ready to roll, and the first research takes us immediately to the book of Acts, where a form of the word shows up twice.

Then Paul stood in the midst of Mars' hill, and said, "Ye men of Athens, I perceive that in all things you are too superstitious. For as I passed by and beheld your devotions, I found an altar with this inscription, TO THE UNKNOWN GOD. Whom therefore you ignorantly worship.
—Acts 17:22–23

But had certain questions against him of their own superstition, and of one Jesus, which was dead, whom Paul affirmed to be alive.
—Acts 25:19

This just tells us these unfounded and mysterious beliefs are nothing new. They date back a couple of thousand years, at least. So, with all that out of the way, let's check out just exactly why Friday the 13th is such a feared and unlucky day. There are all kinds of legends, but the one most readily accepted and agreed upon is that Friday is the day of the Crucifixion of our Lord. This is believable, but then things take a strange turn, and some historians conclude that Adam and

Eve ate the fruit on a Friday. (Don't know about that.) They go on to report the Great Flood started on a Friday. (I know it started on the seventeenth day of the second month, according to Scripture, but whether that was a Friday or not, I can't say.) Yet some continue on and declare it was on a Friday that Cain killed Abel. (These folks have studied their calendar history a lot more than I have, and I'm not sure where they're getting their info.) But the day of the Crucifixion is enough for me to understand how this day gained a place of darkness and dread down through the ages.

Next, why the number thirteen? This one is simple and the only answer to be found is that there were thirteen people at the Last Supper. That fact alone substantiates the word, triskaidekaphobia, meaning the fear of the number thirteen.

Here is one of Paul's experiences in the delusion of sorcery that I have always loved. He and Luke had just shipwrecked and wound up on the island of Malta, about sixty miles south of Sicily. As they came ashore on a cold and rainy day, they found the natives very friendly. They built the two men a fire and made them feel welcome in every way. Paul was up and gathering brushwood to help stoke the campfire when a snake crawled out of his den and latched on to Paul's hand. The natives' attitude toward their guests took a turn, and they said to one another, "Oh, this man must be some sort of murderer or something. The sea didn't get him but this snake will. It will render justice where it's needed. He's a dead man!"

But Paul merely held his hand over the fire, with the snake still hanging to it, and shook it loose. The people of the island sat with open mouths waiting for this stranger to swell up and die. But after a long period, they again changed their minds and declared he must be a god.

They got it wrong again. Paul was flesh and blood but God was in him. Fears and superstitions come from man, but when we turn it over to God, there is neither. The Irish statesman and Christian Edmund Burke (1729–1797) said it better than I ever could:

Religion is the true remedy for superstition.

Lucy Doesn't Like
Daylight Savings Time

Our dog, Lucy, eats dinner every evening at 6 P.M. She never glances at the wall clock in the kitchen, never sets an alarm on the oven, and doesn't even own an Apple watch. But without fail, when the hands of the clock are straight up and down, she goes to the little closet in the corner of the hallway that houses her treats and dog food, and sits, waiting to be noticed and served. Of course, in November when we "fall back" an hour, Lucy's stomach doesn't react to federal demands. It is now five o'clock when she makes her predictable path to the closet door, and no amount of showing her your watch dial or explaining who Benjamin Franklin was will make her budge. She's there for dinner, and she will stare down a twelve-pound Napoleon cannon before she will even blink. Waiting an hour is even more out of the question.

And that's along the lines of what we hear from our farmer friends. The animals get confused. The cows, the chickens, the pigs are all used to eating and sleeping by the sun, and its appearance and disappearance is essential to their schedules. They don't change. Farmer and Mrs. Brown do, but the farm stays on sun time the way God, Hawaii, and Arizona intended it (those are the two states that never change).

Yes, it was our old, Early-American forefather Ben Franklin who suggested the idea of saving daylight to the French. The actual engineering of it came from New Zealand in 1895, but Ben has been the folk hero, or villain, whose name has attached itself to DST down through the years. And whether you are an advocate or an opponent of the idea, you may find it interesting that, according to at least me, the roots of the concept are much deeper and date back to the Old Testament, Joshua, chapter 10, circa 1200 B.C.

Joshua was making quite a name for himself as a warrior and a battle general. He had destroyed the city of Ai and hung their king on a tree. He shouted down the walls of Jericho, killing their king and all those living there. His fame spread causing some to fear him but prompting others to challenge him. Like the gunfighter who had just come to town, he became a target for those in power who wanted to share in his fame and be the one to make him bite the dust.

Five kings—Adoni-Zedek, Hoham, Jarmuth, Japhia, and Debir (don't even try to pronounce them)—joined forces and attacked Gibeon because they knew Joshua and the Israelites had a peace treaty with that city. They were depending on Joshua hearing of their aggression and drawing him out to do battle, and Joshua didn't disappoint them. He got word first from the Gibeonites asking desperately for his help. Next came word from God, who said to him, *"Don't be afraid of them. I have given them into your hand. Not one of them will be able to withstand you"* (Josh. 10:8).

Joshua and his entire army marched all night from Gilgal, where he was camped, to Gibeon, which was under siege of the five kings and their five armies. He made quick work of wiping out the enemy forces and chasing them out of town. The Lord, who had encouraged Joshua and his men into this fray, never took his eye off the battle. As the remaining soldiers of the five kingdoms retreated down the road, running for their lives, God hurled large hailstones on them down from the sky. The Scriptures clearly state "*more of them died from the hailstones than were killed by the swords of the Israelites*" (Josh. 10:11).

And here is where that first decree of Daylight Savings Time came in. In the heat of the battle, seeing that he needed more light to finish the job, Joshua appealed to God, saying:

> "*O sun, stand still over Gibeon, O moon, over the Valley of Aijalon.*"
> *So the sun stood still, and the moon stopped, till the nation avenged itself on its enemies.*
>
> —Joshua 10:12–13

Wouldn't you know it, the sun *did* stop in the middle of the sky and never went down for almost a full day. Just enough time to give Joshua enough light to finish the battle he had started. Not an extra hour of daylight like we get, but an extra *day* of sunlight in answer to the prayer of a faithful soldier.

Warning: don't take issue with Joshua's seemingly archaic understanding of the movements of the sun and the moon. He wasn't a scientist. Now we know the sun doesn't move and that the earth revolves around it. But this was about thirty-two centuries ago, so let's give him a break. And let's not forget our own language, even today, when we talk about "the sun setting" and "the sun rising." Point is, this was a miracle of God.

And I just love the simple and low-key ending to this story in one lone sentence:

> *Then Joshua returned with all Israel to the camp at Gilgal.*
> —Joshua 10:15

We tend to feed Lucy whenever her heart or stomach tells her she's hungry. And that's pretty much how God treats us. He knows what we need and can handle before we do. He calls us for a job, and by his hand and his will, we do it. Then it's on to a new challenge.

Turn your clocks up or back for whatever season and then, like Joshua, *don't be afraid*. Let's be ready for whatever duty God has in store for us next.

It Was Palm Sunday in Syracuse

When The Statlers were touring, Phil and I ran, trotted, or walked every day. Usually not together, but we both were very loyal to it. We rounded parking lots, local parks, side roads, or city streets; just anywhere available and close to the hotel where we were staying. I remember distinctly (and my records show clearly), it was March 28, 1999, in downtown Syracuse. We had a 3 P.M. concert that afternoon but plenty of time to get my daily exercise in. The streets were fairly deserted on a Sunday morning as I walked the blocks, enjoying the spring air and the old buildings which never fail to entertain me. Rounding one corner, I came upon a scene, by an old city church, of children marching and carrying palm leaves. I stopped and watched them and listened to them sing as they placed the branches on the sidewalk in front of them. This was obviously a Sunday school class of seven-year-olds and under, and their teachers were close by for their safety. It was a beautiful sight that I can still see and relive each year, and it always brings a smile to my heart.

I continued my walk in another direction as not to interrupt them, but about thirty minutes later I came back that same way. The block was empty now and quiet. The kids had gone home or back to class, but their palm leaves were still lying about, strewn down the street for all the world to see their handiwork. It was as if Jesus had just ridden by and left a sense of the day, there in our modern world, telling the children it was a job well done. I picked one up and carried it with me for the rest of my walk.

> *A very large crowd spread their cloaks on the road, while others cut branches from the trees and spread them on the road.*
>
> —Matthew 21:8

Why Palm leaves and coats?

Well, the palm leaves, by this time in Jewish history, had become a symbol of victory, respect, and worship. The book of Leviticus explains the meaning of the tree branches that bear the fruit of the date.

> *On the first day, you are to take choice fruit from the trees, and palm fronds, leafy branches and poplars, and rejoice before the Lord your God for seven days.*
>
> —Leviticus 23:40

And it was a seemingly victorious entrance as Jesus rode into Jerusalem on the back of a donkey, a symbol of peace. A warrior would have ridden in on horseback. This ecstatic crowd, still expecting an earthly king, took off their coats and lay them, along with the fronds, in his path, just as men had done for King Jehu some 840 years before.

> *They hurried and took their cloaks and spread them under him on the bare steps. Then they blew the trumpet and shouted, "Jehu is King!"*
>
> —2 Kings 9:13

I heard an actor, Walter Pidgeon, whom most won't recognize today, recite a poem on a late-night television show when I was a very young man. I loved that poem and searched bookstores, old and new, for half a lifetime looking for it, though I didn't even know the title. I only knew it was about a donkey and that it gave me chills when I heard it that first and only time. The day of discovery came a quarter of a century later in a dusty, old antique store/bookshop in Debbie's hometown of Milan, Tennessee. I stood there, dumbfounded and thankful, and read the words of "The Donkey" by G. K. Chesterton for the first time.

Told from the viewpoint of the donkey himself, the opening verses are spent relating how ugly a creature he is, how sickening his bray, how dumb, with a monstrous head and enormous ears. Then comes the final verse, which says it all:

Fools! For I also had my hour
One far fierce hour and sweet;
There was a shout about my ears
And palms before my feet

Holy Week, the week between Palm Sunday and Easter, carries more emotion and mood changes than can be imagined in most lifetimes. Jesus went from being an arriving hero to being publicly executed in five days. Within those few short days, the cries of the crowd went from "Hosanna!" to "Crucify him!" And that donkey he chose, who had never been ridden by another human, carried him gallantly and loyally into the Holy City with palms before his feet.

It's Palm Sunday. The King has arrived.

Serpent in a Glass Jar

It was a serpent that began the Fall of Man. A serpent that reared its ugly head to come between God and mankind. A serpent that caused all the problems that are still felt in the world today. And it was a serpent that rolled down the hall in a glass jar that fateful day in high school and burst against the wall, bringing me even more love and respect for my mother. Let me start at the beginning.

A sophomore at Wilson Memorial High, somewhere back in 1960, I was walking down a hallway when a large glass jar came rolling from the doorway of the science lab, past me, heading for heaven only knows where. But before it reached its target destination, if indeed there was one, it veered slightly, hit a brick column, and spewed formaldehyde and glass all over the west end of the corridor. It also left a large dead snake lying in the center of the walkway. A few of us watched, laughed, and went on to class, as fourteen-year-olds are wont to do.

Ten minutes later, I was called to the office over the intercom system. The principal was waiting at the door and informed me it had been reported I had witnessed the "snake episode," and he wanted me to give him the name of the person who was responsible. In all honesty, I had seen who threw the jar, but being a casual friend of the boy, I decided

I wasn't going to rat him out. Mr. Principal did not take kindly to my refusal and instructed me to find a seat in the office and remain there until I agreed to offer him the information he demanded. When the three o'clock bell rang that afternoon to dismiss school, he told me to report back to the office the next morning and to be prepared to sit there every day until I relented.

It was during casual conversation at the supper table that evening when I told my parents what had taken place that day at school. The only question my mother asked was, "Don't you have six-weeks' tests this week?"

"All week long," I replied.

At 9 A.M. sharp the next morning, I looked out the window from the little room beside the principal's office where I was perched for the day, and saw Mom pull up and get out of the car. She came in, asked for Mr. Principal by name, and I could overhear every word of their conversation.

"I want my son back in class as he is missing all of his six-weeks' tests."

"But Mrs. Reid, he knows who threw that snake down the hall."

"Do you have reason to believe *he* did it?"

"We know *he* didn't do it but he knows who did, and he's staying where he is until he tells me."

"I didn't raise him to be a tattletale. If I knew, I wouldn't tell you either. So, if you know he didn't do it, I want him back in class immediately."

From my window, I saw her exit the backdoor of the office, get in her car, and drive away. The next voice I heard was from Mr. Principal standing in the doorway, glaring at me, saying, "Reid. Get back in class."

That was my mom. Her life and her actions were full of little lessons I carry with me today. She never boasted about what she was going to do before she did it, nor did she gloat after the fact. She simply did what was on her heart in the fairest and most succinct way possible. I don't remember that we ever talked about this incident afterwards, and she never had a critical word to say about the principal in any way. She realized he was just trying to do his job but also that she had a job to do as a mother. Had I been the guilty one that busted the snake jar, she would have been on Mr. P's side and I would have been in trouble aplenty. But I wasn't and she wasn't and I wasn't.

> *Hear, my son, your father's instruction, and forsake not your mother's teaching.*
> —Proverbs 1:8

By the way, the guy who threw the "snake in the jar" never thanked me for keeping his secret. And the principal, twenty years later, pitched me some songs he had written for The Statlers to record.

Every lesson in life is full of surprises.

The Journey

We all know the real reason they went. It was foretold in the book of Micah some 750 years before it happened:

> *But you, Bethlehem Ephrathah, though you are small among the clans of Judah, out of you will come for me one who will be ruler over Israel, whose origins are from old, from ancient times.*
>
> *—Micah 5:2*

The earthly reason is given in the book of Luke:

> *In those days Caesar Augustus issued a decree that a census should be taken of the entire Roman world. (This was the first census that took place while Quirinius was governor of Syria.) And everyone went to his own town to register. So, Joseph also went up from the town of Nazareth in Galilee to Judea, to Bethlehem the town of David, because he belonged to the house and line of David. He went there to register with Mary, who was pledged to be married to him and was expecting a child.*
>
> *—Luke 2:1–5*

And that is all we're told in the Bible about their journey.

Mary and Joseph were living in Nazareth, in Galilee, a town of about 1,400 people. Some sources say approximately two hundred families lived there, making seven the average family. Sounds about right, as we know Jesus grew up in a family of at least nine (four brothers, at least two sisters, and his parents). There are a number of ways they could have traveled to Bethlehem. They could have walked the distance, ridden in a cart, or ridden a donkey or horse, but the truth is, we just don't know. What we do know is that their destination was sixty miles due south as the crow flies. But herein lies the problem. That straight route would take them through the heart of Samaria, and we know the dubious relationship between Jews and Samaritans of that time. Remember the parable of the Good Samaritan? This was very unfriendly country, and you didn't want to travel through there with your wife if you were a Jew. The alternative and best route, for a couple of reasons, would be a little southeast, down around the Jordan River.

The first reason, of course, was safety. The second was the availability of the water they would need for themselves and their animals because this was not an overnight trip. Going this way was one hundred miles, and historians have figured that covering a little more than sixteen miles a day, this would be a six-day trip. And that is a pretty tough journey when you're nine months pregnant, facing the desert, rough terrain, mountain lions, snakes, and bandits.

On the sixth and final day of their trip, they came into the big city of Jerusalem. The New York City of Judea. As they did, they would have to pass, on the main road, right by the scene of half-buried crosses in the sand where public crucifixions took place. Without knowing it, they were seeing the site of Jesus' death before seeing the site of his birth.

Don Reid

Israel in the time of Jesus

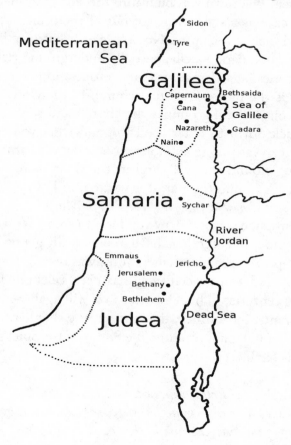

Bethlehem (Ephrathah, in the Scriptures, was the district near and around the city—think county) was only five miles farther. The town was built into the side of a ridge, so utilizing a cave as a stable was not out of the ordinary, but rather very much in the norm. Not a cute little barn out back, but a cold, dank, dark, smelly, partially underground cavern. Three centuries later, Emperor Constantine and his mother built what is the oldest Christian church in the world over this site. You can still go under the church and see it. You have to duck down to enter the cave, and what you see is about fourteen yards long and four yards wide. It's lighted by silver lamps around the wall, and in the floor there is engraved a star. Around the star, it is written, in Latin:

Here Jesus Christ was born of the Virgin Mary

The entrance way is so low you have to stoop. You have to bend in order to enter. You have to practically get on your knees to approach the place where Jesus was born.

This sacred and peaceful day has been celebrated and revered for centuries. This Christmas we will again remember the parents, the journey, the manger, the shepherds, the wise men, but most importantly, the Son, and the quiet small town of his birth.

O little town of Bethlehem, how still we see thee lie
Above they deep and dreamless sleep, the silent stars go by
Yet in thy dark street shineth, the everlasting light
The hopes and fears of all the years are met in the thee
 tonight

"O Little Town of Bethlehem"
—Phillips Brooks

Paying Taxes

Peter played an integral role in Jesus' three-year ministry. He was personally involved in many of the teaching stories related about Jesus in the four Gospels, and not just by being one of the Twelve. In many of the stories, we are privy to the personal relationship between the two men. A perfect example is the story of the temple tax.

Of course, the Jewish powers that be were constantly trying to discredit Jesus in any way they could. Their numerous charges were never able to stick, but that didn't keep them from digging up some new trouble for him wherever they could find it. They hung the charge of blasphemy on him, saying he claimed to be the son of God. They tried to prove him a criminal when he healed the sick on the Sabbath. And finding nothing that could turn the people against him, they finally resorted to tax evasion. Strangely, Matthew is the only one of the Gospel writers who tells this story, but Peter, as he always seemed to be, was right in the middle of it.

An annual temple tax of two drachma (half a shekel) was required of the public. This law was not enforceable by the Roman government, but the Jewish priests insisted on its payment during the Passover. One of the collectors approached Peter face-to-face and asked him, "Doesn't your teacher pay the temple tax?"

Without hesitation, and apparently without too much thought, Peter answered, "Yes, he does."

Later, when Peter came into the house where Jesus was staying, the Scriptures tell us Jesus was the first to speak, and he said, "What do you think, Simon? From whom do the kings of the earth collect duty and taxes—from their own sons or from others?"

Peter replied, "From others."

"Then the sons are exempt," Jesus said to him. "But so that we may not offend them, go to the lake and throw out your line. Take the first fish you catch; open its mouth and you will find a four-drachma coin. Take it and give it to them for your tax and mine."

So many interesting points in this short story. Note that the Scripture (Matt. 17:24–27) makes a point of telling us that when Peter entered the house, Jesus was the first to speak. Peter didn't tell him about the conversation with the collectors about the tax, but Jesus already knew all about it. Such a subtle way of telling us that he knows all things and nothing is kept from him.

And then let's consider quick-tongued Peter, who spoke right up and gave false information when he was asked if Jesus paid his temple tax. Many think Jesus not only paid the tax so he wouldn't offend the Jewish leaders, but also to save Peter's integrity and honor.

And the final point is that the four-drachma coin covered just Jesus' and Peter's obligation to the temple—not that of the other eleven. Again, this reflects a certain show of the closeness between these two—the Teacher and the disciple.

But maybe the defining story of this man Peter's involvement with the earthly Jesus is the one best known. Jesus was on the mountainside, alone, praying while the Twelve were out in a boat a good distance from shore. Night came and the wind was up and the waves became rough, but Jesus, wanting to board the boat with his disciples, walked across the lake to meet them. When they saw him on the water, they were scared and yelled out, "It's a ghost!"

Jesus calmed them all down and told them not to be afraid. But when Peter saw him, he said, "Lord, if it's you, tell me to come to you on the water."

"Come," Jesus said.

At this, Peter climbed out of the boat and became the only other person besides Jesus himself to walk on water. But as he walked toward him, the high wind scared Peter and he started to sink and cried out, "Lord, save me!"

And Jesus did. He reached out his hand and caught him. And the lesson is there for us all. As long as we're walking toward Jesus, he will always reach out and take us to where he wants us to be. Storms, high winds, and waves of life won't keep him from it.

QUESTION FOR THOUGHT

What was the temple tax of two drachma per person worth in our currency today?

ANSWER

There is more than one way to answer this question. What was the gold in the coins worth in today's market, or what was the tax worth in today's market? The relevant answer here is the latter, at approximately sixty-five cents.

From a Child

Sometimes I hear stories I tell myself I'm going to remember and share because they make me laugh or have a real poignant meaning, but then I wind up forgetting them before the day is over. Other times, those stories stick and I find myself revisiting them and thinking about them years later. This is one of the latter. I wasn't there firsthand, but this happened to a friend of mine a number of years ago while on vacation.

He and his six-year-old daughter were on the beach one afternoon. She had a bucket and a matching shovel and was digging in the sand for what he called "moonfish." As she was putting them in her little beach bucket, two ladies who were walking down the beach together stopped to see what she was doing. One of the ladies, in exclamation, said, "My God, look how many fish you have!"

His little girl, never looking up from her digging, said, "You shouldn't use God's name like that."

The lady, in disbelief and with a puzzled looked, said, "What's that you say?"

The little girl, still digging, replied, "You shouldn't use God's name like that. It's not nice."

The lady looked at her friend beside her, motioned toward the girl, and said, "What is she talking about?"

The second lady rolled her eyes, took her friend by the arm, whispered, and said, "They're Christians."

"Oh," said the first lady, and the two of them walked on down the beach.

This beautiful yet ugly story could go in two directions at this point. I could launch into a heavy topic in a preachy way about the third commandment and what it means to us in everyday life. I could point out all the ways we abuse said commandment and misuse God's name. I could even reprint the commandment here one more time for everyone to see:

Thou shall not take the name of the Lord thy God in vain; for the Lord will not hold him guiltless that taketh his name in vain.

—Exodus 20:7

Then I could offer a dictionary definition of the word vain: *without proper respect; to no purpose.* And then point out that in the disrespectful and impertinent world we live in today, social media has even given us an initialism, OMG, right at our fingertips to make it easier for everyone to offend at any moment, day or night.

But that is not what I'm going to do. That's not the direction we're going to take. To me, the story is not so much about what this unthinking, uninformed adult said and did, but about what this sweet and innocent six-year-old said and did. With no rancor or malice, this little girl continued to have fun in the sand and at the same time speak her heart about what she had learned in Sunday school and, more importantly, what she had been taught at home. There was never a question in her mind if she should defend God's name. If she should speak up on his behalf. If she might offend the one who had just offended. And I dare say, many of us adults would not have handled it in any better manner.

I'm afraid we might have remained silent and just ignored the lady's insulting words. That's what we do in order to survive in today's society. We try to avoid confrontation and conflict even when we know we're in the right. And I'm not even saying that is a bad thing. I'm just saying we can learn so much from watching the innocence and love of the children around us. Bless them, everyone.

> *Verily I say unto you, whosoever shall not receive the kingdom of God as a little child shall in no wise enter therein.*
>
> —Luke 18:17

A Man Through the Roof

When I was a kid, my favorite Bible story was the one where they let the man down through the roof on a mattress and Jesus healed him. Then the man got up, put his bed under his arm, and walked out through the crowd. I remember we acted this story out in Bible school one year, and this is exactly how I pictured the story and remembered it. It wasn't until I reread it many times as an adult that the content and meaning of the story took on so much more. Yes, Jesus healed a paralyzed man who had been lowered through the ceiling of a room, and yes, this man got up and walked out a new and renewed human being. But isn't it amazing how one fascinating story can attract a child and that same story can mean so much more to a hungry and searching adult?

Mark (2:1–12) and Luke (5:17–26) wrote about this same story with very little difference in their telling. Jesus, by this time in his ministry, had left Nazareth and was living in Capernaum. Peter was from there, and John, James, Andrew, and Matthew also lived in this small fishing village. Jesus had come home for a stay, and when the locals heard he was there, so many gathered in and around his house to hear him teach and talk that not another person could get near him.

Four men arrived carrying their disabled friend on a mat, hoping Jesus would heal him. When they couldn't get into the house, instead of giving up and saying to one another, "Well, at least we tried," they took him up to the roof and proceeded to dig up a portion of the top of the house until they had a hole big enough to accommodate the man and the mat. They lowered him down right in front of Jesus. And this is where my new understanding of the story as an adult really kicks in:

> *When Jesus saw their faith, he said to the paralyzed man, "Son, your sins are forgiven."*
> —Mark 2:5

So many times in the New Testament, Jesus says to someone he has just made whole, "Your faith has healed you." And this time, he not only acknowledged the faith of the sick man, but he "saw *their* faith." He saw the love and faith of those four friends who carried the man to the house. Then carried him to the roof, which could not have been an easy task, even if there were steps leading to it. Then dug up a tight and secure roof. And then lowered him down into the crowd, interrupting Jesus' message. These weren't casual acquaintances. These were four good, loyal, and loving friends who didn't just ask, "What can I do to help?" They took ahold of the situation and took advantage of Jesus being at home and truly believed that their friend could and would be healed and be able to walk away from that house that day. They pushed and persevered and let nothing stand in their way to get their friend the healing he needed from the only person in heaven or earth who could do it. *Their* faith was what Jesus saw and reacted to. And because of the faith of all five of these friends, the Scriptures tell us:

> *He got up, took his mat and walked out in full view of them all. This amazed everyone and they praised God saying, "We have never seen anything like this!"*
> —Mark 2:12

We all love and cherish that wonderful verse from John 15:13—*Greater love hath no man than this, that a man lay down his life for his friends.* Life was not involved here, but these men offered up their faith for their friend. They stepped up for him when he needed them. They took a day off from work and took him to Jesus. They carried him and lowered him and watched him be healed. Jesus saw their faith and recognized their sincerity. And sometime this week, I pray he'll see yours and mine. And maybe someone else will, too, and then they will be inspired to show theirs. And that's the way Jesus passes through this old world, touching each believer as he goes.

> *My faith looks up to thee*
> *Thou lamb of calvary*
> *Savior divine*
> *Now hear me while I pray*
> *Take all my guilt away*
> *O let me from this day*
> *Be wholly thine*
> "My Faith Looks Up to Thee"
> —Ray Palmer

Eutychus

Have you ever fallen asleep in church? Maybe just a nod or two? Or maybe a full-out, no-holds-barred Sunday-morning nap? A friend once told me he saw a man inconspicuously go to sleep during a church service while sitting straight up in the pew. His head didn't bob, he didn't snore, and no one around him, except this friend of mine, was even aware the man had taken leave of the world for a few restful minutes. Not until he woke up, yawned big and loud, and stretched both arms in the air while arching his back. At this point, *every*one knew and would never forget it.

The ultimate story of falling asleep in church during a sermon happened to Paul. It was on the first day of the week, a Sunday, and Paul was in Troas, Turkey. The church there had gathered for a meal, as all churches will, at the drop of a salad fork or the mention of a casserole. Afterwards, as is still the custom, they needed an after-dinner speaker, and that honor went to the visiting Paul. Because he was leaving the next day, he wanted to take this opportunity to say every-thing on his heart to these folks, so like the engrossed orator he was, he just kept on and on talking. Come midnight, he was still at it.

The meeting at which Paul was speaking was held in an upstairs room that was full of lamps to provide light for this ongoing sermon that had lasted until after dark, and now well beyond. Seated in one of the windows of this third-story meeting house was a young man named Eutychus. We are never told his age, so we can never know just exactly how young he was. As Paul's sermon grew longer and longer, Eutychus grew drowsier by the minute and finally fell asleep and out the window. Yes! He fell three stories to the ground. The people rushed down the steps and out the door to offer their help and assistance, but all were too late. Eutychus was dead.

Paul, the apostle, pushed through the crowd and took charge immediately. He threw himself on top of the young man, put his arms around him, and hugged him. Looking up and speaking to all who were standing there, he said, "Don't be alarmed. He's alive!"

At this point, the entire congregation went back up-stairs; they all got something to eat, and Paul continued to preach until daylight. Then...*Then* they took Eutychus home. He had stayed all night for the eating and preaching even after being raised from the dead.

This is the true purpose of the story. The young man was certainly and surely dead when the people found him lying on the ground. Luke, the author of Acts, where this story is found, was himself a physician and an eyewitness. So, if Luke says he wasn't breathing, we have to believe he wasn't. This miracle gives supreme credibility to Paul, who now becomes only the fifth person in all history to actually raise someone from the dead.

I never read or hear this story that I don't think of our dad. To understand it completely, you have to know that he was a "character." Our mother was the moral pillar of faith and attendance in our family, and Dad, bless his heart, often fell through the cracks from time to time. And I say that with nothing but a heart full of love and laughter for him. A family story that happened before I was born tells of his relationship with our minister, Rev. Lowman.

After not seeing him in the family pew for a number of weeks, Mr. Lowman stopped our dad one day on the street and said, "Haven't seen you at church in a while, Sidney. Where have you been?"

"Been working the graveyard shift at DuPont," Dad replied. "I don't get home till nearly 8 A.M., and I'm afraid if I come to church, I'll fall asleep right smack dab in the middle of your sermon."

Mr. Lowman patted him on the back and said, "That's alright, Sid. At least I'll know where you are."

Mr. Lowman had Dad's number, and Paul had Eutychus's back. But we all know who did it. We all know who brought the young man back from the dead and who saw that our dad was in church every Sunday for the last ten years of his life.

Now, who was looking out for that fellow who yawned out loud and stretched real big when he woke up in the middle of the morning service, I can't say. But I sure do wish I'd been there to see it.

Imperfect

Some people strive all their lives to be perfect. Even as kids, they put too much pressure on themselves and carry the weight of the world on their shoulders. As students, they work into the night for the highest grade in the class. As adults, they want to overachieve and are destroyed by the slightest bump in the road. And some of this is good, but we have to realize even God doesn't expect us to be unblemished in all we do. If he did, we'd still be living under the law. But he knows our weaknesses. He knows, above all others, that we are not perfect.

Mark tells a story over in the ninth chapter about a man with imperfect faith. A father brings his son to Jesus, which shows he has a certain amount of the right faith. He tells Jesus the boy is regularly tormented by a demon. This horrible spirit has robbed the boy completely of his speech. It grabs him and throws him down on the ground. It causes him to foam at the mouth, gnash his teeth, and makes his body become rigid like a board. The father said to Jesus, "I asked your disciples to drive out the evil spirit but they couldn't do it."

"Bring the boy to me," Jesus told him.

When he brought his son, the spirit saw Jesus and recognized him. It immediately threw the boy on the ground and into a convulsion, making him roll around violently and foam at the mouth.

"How long has he been like this?" Jesus asked calmly.

"From childhood," the man answered with sadness in his voice. "It often throws him into fire or water and tries to kill him."

And here is where the imperfect faith comes in. The father says to Jesus, "If you can do anything, take pity on us and help us."

"If you can?" Jesus asks as an emphasis. He speaks the same words back to the man in the form of a question. "If you can?" Surely, the man was brought to reality by Jesus' tone. And surely, he felt his forgiving nature when Jesus said, "Everything is possible for him who believes."

The desperate father, now realizing his weakness and imperfection, pleaded with Jesus and said, "I do believe. Help me overcome my unbelief."

Jesus commanded the spirit, "Come out of him and never enter him again."

The demon convulsed him one more time, then shrieked and came out. The boy lay on the ground like a corpse until Jesus took him by the hand and lifted him to his feet.

Jesus didn't walk away from a needy and helpless father and leave his son in misery. He wasn't offended by the man's lack of faith. Instead, he saw the glimmer of faith in him and acted on it. And he does the same for us every day of our lives. The Bible is full of saints with imperfections. Thomas doubted. Moses tried to get out of his mission. Abraham laughed in God's face. Peter denied him. And we could go on and on. All of these stalwarts of the Old and New

Testaments were just as much in need as the next one. Just like you. Just like me.

The perfect postscript to this story comes when Jesus was alone again with the disciples. Maybe a little embarrassed, perhaps a little puzzled, they said to him, "Why couldn't *we* drive that spirit out?"

He replied, "This kind can come out only by prayer."

Prayer is the key to heaven, but faith unlocks the door.
"Faith Unlocks the Door"
—Samuel Scott/Robert Sande

And the Home of the Brave

Francis Scott Key was born in Fredrick, Maryland, about two and a half hours up the road from us here in Staunton. He got his law degree and moved to Georgetown to set up practice. This is where life found him when the War of 1812 broke out. Key was also a very devout and active layman in the Episcopal church. It was through his church that he made friends with Dr. William Beanes, a local physician.

During a siege of Baltimore in 1814, the British took American prisoners aboard their boats, and among them was Dr. Beanes. President James Madison, knowing Francis Scott Key to be a good lawyer, a seasoned negotiator, and a friend of Beanes, sent him on a truce ship in pursuit of the British. His objective was to safely rescue his friend and all the others, if possible. They followed the enemy ship into the harbor of Baltimore, which would be in the area of Camden Yards where the Orioles play baseball today. The British army, with other ships, attacked Baltimore, and Key watched the battle all night long. He paced the deck of the truce ship and saw the bombs and rockets light up the darkness and held his ears as each battle noise blasted into the sky. This went on until the morning sun was just coming up enough for him to see the damage all around him. The first thing he saw, though, looking into the harbor, was the American flag. Still standing. Still flying.

Weary, tired, and exhausted from no sleep, Key felt in his pocket and found an envelope and wrote on the back, in the gray light of dawn, these words. Take a moment and read them. Not as a poem. Not as a song. But as a story you have never heard before. Then feel the power of the picture he paints.

O say can you see, by the dawn's early light
What so proudly we hailed at the twilight's last gleaming
Whose broad stripes and bright stars, through the perilous
*   fight*
O'er the ramparts we watched, were so gallantly streaming
And the rockets' red glare, the bombs bursting in air
Gave proof through the night, that our flag was still there
O say does that star-spangled banner yet wave
O'er the land of the free, and the home of the brave

Dr. William Beanes was rescued and lived to be an old man and practice medicine the rest of his life. Francis Scott Key would become the district attorney of Washington, DC, and argue numerous cases before the Supreme Court. And that flag, peeping through the morning fog after a hard night's battle, would survive and flourish for many, many generations to come. F. Scott Key would find fame in those words he wrote that hot, late-summer night out there on the harbor on September 14, 1814. He would borrow a melody from an old English drinking song called "To Anacreon in Heaven" to fit the words of his poem, and he would go down in history as the writer of one of the most famous songs ever written.

But it wasn't for another 117 years that Congress would legally make it our National Anthem on March 3, 1931.

Then conquer we must, when our cause it is just
And this be our motto, in God we trust
And the star-spangled banner, in triumph shall wave
O'er the land of the free, and the home of the brave

Being Worthy

If you have ever served on a nominating committee at your church where your duty is to ask fellow members to serve in some capacity, I'm sure you've heard all the reasons and excuses to decline numerous times. Right-minded and good-hearted people try hard to give you an answer that won't offend you and won't make them feel guilty. What they're searching for is a way of giving you a gentle but firm "No." The most oft-heard one is, of course, "I don't have the time." And I have to believe this. Church duties do often take time away from a daily schedule, consist of evening meetings, and have Sunday-morning obligations. I know there is possible sincerity in such an answer, and I respect someone who wants to make a full commitment should they take on an active obligation.

The second most often heard is "Not this time. Ask me again next year." Well, this is just putting off the inevitable answer. It's like young married couples saying, "We're waiting to have children when we can afford them." News flash for the young marrieds: it doesn't work that way. If we all had waited until we could afford to get married and afforded kids and afforded a house and afforded a car, we'd be living somewhere today in a tent by ourselves and riding a skateboard to work. At some point you just have to jump in and do it!

The honest and open answer that serves best is "I'm not sure I'm ready. I'm going to pray about it." This is what we all should do when we are feeling any reservation about making a commitment. God knows when we're ready to serve and knows in what way we can best perform. There's a place for everyone and it's just finding the right fit.

The most difficult answer I have ever heard came from an older gentleman who was known to be one of the most studious in the congregation. He knew the Bible from creation to Revelation and was active in Sunday school and every Bible study anyone held. He knew all the answers when others struggled with them. He was gentle and kind and could easily, without pride, quote the proper verse for any situation that might come up in any discussion. But when asked to serve as a church officer, his annual answer was the same: "No. I'm not worthy."

And who is going to argue with that? None of us are ever worthy. But we serve when we're called and the Holy Scriptures are full of these illustrations. Take Peter and bro Andrew, for example.

> *As* Jesus *was walking beside the Sea of Galilee, he saw two brothers, Simon called Peter and his brother Andrew. They were casting a net into the lake, for they were fishermen. "Come, follow me," Jesus said, "and I will send you out to fish for people." At once they left their nets and followed him.*
> —Matthew 4:18–20

Do you think Peter knew when he got up that morning and went to work his whole life was going to be changed? Do you think he even considered hollering back at Jesus and saying, "Not this time, Master? Ask me again next year."

Going on from there, he saw two other brothers, James son of Zebedee and his brother John. They were in a boat with their father Zebedee, preparing their nets. Jesus called them, and immediately they left the boat and their father and followed him.

—Matthew 4:21–22

Immediately they left their boat and their father with no apparent explanation. Just dropped what they were doing and walked into a new life of service. This kind of committing to what you believe is so very deep that it just muddles the mind and swells the heart.

I could go on, but we all know the stories. The warning is to be ready because we never know what we may be asked to do. And if Jesus is expecting a "Yes," we don't want to disappoint him.

But be sure to fear the Lord and serve him faithfully with all your heart; consider what great things he has done for you.

—1 Samuel 12:24

These People Are Not Drunk

Theologians and scholars for centuries have believed that the book of Mark was, in essence, the book of Peter. It is believed that Peter may actually have dictated the book to Mark or was his main source of personal reference. So many things are accredited to Peter and told through his eyes that his influence on the eldest Gospel is hard to ignore. This is strange and potentially confusing since when we get further over into the New Testament, many believe that maybe Peter didn't actually write the books of 1 and 2 Peter. But so be the mysteries of the Holy Scriptures. Often, it isn't so important who wrote what, but that it was written for our benefit and understanding. And did I say Mark's book was the eldest of the Gospels? Well, that stands in contention also, and many researchers put in their vote for Matthew. But after all is read and done, does any of this back-and-forth really matter? It still remains, for all generations and for all believers, the word of God.

With that said, we are pretty certain that it was Luke who wrote the book of Acts. And we can credit him with giving us some rich and insightful history concerning Peter. Until this time, we have known Peter as a follower, a disciple, and a believer in Christ throughout the four Gospels. But it is only a little way into the book of Acts that we see him in a new, strong, and independent light. The day of Pentecost (the Greek word for fifty, thus, fifty days after Easter), sees Peter in full charge. The Holy Spirit has just been bestowed upon the new twelve disciples in Jerusalem, and they all begin speaking in tongues. Jews from every nation who hear them are astounded that they can hear them speaking in their own individual language. But there were a few who made fun of them and said, "They have had too much to drink!" And that is when Peter stood, quieted the crowd, and raised his voice. He set the record straight, and in doing so, gave the first Christian sermon after the Ascension that is on record.

> *Fellow Jews and all of you who live in Jerusalem, let me explain this to you; listen carefully to what I say. These people are not drunk, as you suppose. It's only nine in the morning!*
>
> —Acts 2:14–15

Then he proceeded to tell them who Jesus was and is and encouraged them to repent and be baptized, and that very day, the Scriptures tell us, three thousand were saved. Consider that staggering number for a moment. Our church, Olivet, seats 290 folks at full capacity. So, fill it ten times over again with new believers, and that gives us an idea of the extent and power that took place on that day of Pentecost.

Luke was a Gentile and not an eyewitness to what he was reporting, and thus some Christian academics through the ages have thought he was confusing speaking in tongues with speaking with foreign tongues. Not for me to say, but I can tell you that I have witnessed glossolalia (speaking in tongues), as some of you may have, also.

When we, The Statlers, were just teenagers singing around at local churches on Sunday nights, we were invited to sing a few songs at a Pentecostal church just down the road a piece. Being raised in the relatively quiet and sedate Presbyterian faith, it was where I heard my first "Amen" during a sermon. I took that fairly well—a little wide-eyed and startled—but the best was yet to come. When we stood to pray, everyone in the congregation prayed out loud and in their own adopted spiritual tongue. Neither John Knox nor John Calvin had prepared me for any of this, and I found myself staring at the floor and mostly at my watch for the rest of the evening. But we left there that night with a new experience in our hearts and a new respect for the way other folks worship. God bless us all.

I do remember that it took this young teenager to the Bible the next day looking for answers to what I had just witnessed. I found comfort and a better understanding from Paul in 1 Corinthians 14. Take a few quiet moments today and read that entire chapter. A very fitting passage for Pentecost Sunday.

And this is where I so miss our Sunday-morning gatherings in person, because this is where I would love to hear anyone's personal experience with tongues and the effect it had on you at the time. There are many who grew up in other denominations that embrace this practice, many who have a better understanding of it than I do, and I am always interested in learning more about the different ways people worship.

This day of Pentecost was the beginning of Peter's ministry that Jesus had so well prepared him for. This was the beginning of the Church as we know it.

QUESTION FOR THOUGHT

Pentecost Sunday is known by another name in many Christian churches in England, Ireland, and other countries. What is that name?

ANSWER

Whit Sunday, which is short for White Sunday, so called because of an early church custom of wearing white garments when being baptized.

After Thanksgiving Dinner

The fourth Thursday in November is coming close to being the number-one answer when you survey family, friends, or strangers as to their favorite holiday of the year. Mind you, it's still second to Christmas, but there is a lot of charm for a lot of people about this day set aside for giving thanks. I've asked lots of folks who sing the praises of Thanksgiving Day just why they favor it so much, and here are some of the reasons I constantly hear.

1. Noncommercial. No hassle, no harm. No getting beat over the head with schedules and parties and long weeks of preparation.

2. No Gifts. This is a relief to not only the old wallet but to the heart rate. No worry about what the kids want or don't want. No last-minute shopping, no after-Thanksgiving exchanges.

3. No Pressure. The only person under pressure is the one in the kitchen doing the cooking. This is still most likely the wife/mother, but I know of families where dad steps up and shows his culinary talents this one day of the year. The rest of the fam is lounging in the den, falling asleep to the tune of their favorite football teams.

4. Just Being Together. This is undeniable. It is *the* day for family gatherings. Some are small, but some include all the branches of brothers and sisters, aunts and uncles, grandparents, and plenty of kids to keep it lively. Who could not love that kind of circus?

5. The Beginning of the Season. Okay, I added that one myself, because to me, T Day kicks off the Christmas season for the next four weeks. Everything from here on is festive and decorative, and everyone's in an especially good mood. Invitations abound and you visit with, and are visited by, folks you haven't seen all year long.

And there is never a more relaxed time than that after-dinner-push-back-from-the table time while everyone is still sitting and talking. This is when our family starts the holiday season. Our gang is a game family. (There are a couple who aren't, but they humor the rest of us.) A few years ago, when the grandkids were still kids, I made a tradition of having a quiz around the table for everyone. I made up questions suitable for the young and old alike. Such as:

> *If you could have named yourself, what would your first two names be?*
> *Who was your favorite teacher and why?*
> *What's your favorite Christmas song and why?*

It is amazing how long we sometimes sit at the table. Everyone answers their questions and tells their stories, and before you know it, we're ready for another round of pumpkin, pecan, and mincemeat pie.

> *What is something you'd like to learn to do but never have?*
> *What person, living today, would you most like to meet?*

History tells us that the first Thanksgiving, when the New Americans and the Native Americans met, in 1621, and feasted, went on for three days. We don't sit at the table quite that long, but we are never in a rush. All of the family, young, old, and even the teens, linger and seem to enjoy the stories and the opportunity to tell theirs. Who couldn't like answering:

Would you rather eat dinner with three people you don't like or three people who don't like you? Explain.

Would you rather eat cranberry sauce every meal for a month or wear a Pilgrim costume everywhere you go for a week?

The word thanksgiving shows up thirty times in the Bible. It shows up a lot at our house, and we love every minute of it!

Out of them shall come songs of thanksgiving, and the voices of those who celebrate.
> —Jeremiah 30:19

Properly Dressed

There was a time when I was much more conscientious about dressing properly than I am today. There was a place to wear a tie and a place to never wear a tie. It was just as important to never underdress as it was to never overdress. I would never wear khakis to church or a business meeting. And then, I would never wear a suit and tie to a family gathering for dinner. There were set things to wear to set events. But today, all that has enmeshed and tangled to where no one is sure anymore of what is "proper dress" and what is "whatever you're comfortable in" dress.

The women started it. They quit wearing hats to church and started wearing pantsuits. They brought it down a notch to a dressy casual that fit every occasion. Then the men jumped in there and spoiled it all with something called a "leisure suit," and that just crashed the market on taste and boundaries. Before you knew it, there were sport coats at funerals and open collars at weddings. Fashion had taken a hit from which it would never recover. I have even seen shorts at funerals and t-shirts at weddings, and although it makes me cringe, I can only look at myself and see that I'm not the stickler for the proper dress I once was. I am not, understand, guilty of these extremes I have just listed here, but I do find myself at church with no tie (sorry, Mom) and sometimes a sport coat and tie when there is just a graveside service.

Wherever we may fall on a trendy-dress spectrum, it may do us all good to be aware of something the Lord said to Samuel back centuries ago on the matter of King Saul:

> *Do not consider his appearance or his height.... The Lord does not look at the things man looks at. Man looks at the outward appearance, but the Lord looks at the heart.*
>
> —1 Samuel 16:7

This may be good news for us or it may be bad. That's something each of us is going to have to decide for ourselves.

As a kid, I had everyday clothes, school clothes, and Sunday clothes. And never shall the trio meet! No dress pants at school. No new pants at home. And no jeans at church. No sneakers at home unless they had a hole in them or were beginning to get too little. No leather shoes at school. And no (even brand-new) sneakers at church. And the list goes on. So, it's no wonder we may have dress issues as the styles of the day change and the world grows more relaxed. I'm certainly guilty of a more nonchalant, laid-back fashion at church today than I ever have been in my life. There is a story I must share with you about a good friend at Olivet and an incident that happened in recent years.

My friend and I were standing in the vestibule talking before church one Sunday morning when someone approached and reminded us both that we were serving Communion at the end of the worship service. We each thanked him and continued on with our conversation, but I could see his mind was suddenly someplace else. Then he said, "Look at me. I have on khakis, a sport coat, and an open-collar shirt. I can't serve Communion this way."

At this point, he turned abruptly and went out the front door. He drove home, changed into a dark suit and tie, and was back in ample time to take his place at the front of the sanctuary. I tell his story here because I so admire a man who has such respect for God and the sanctity of the Lord's Supper that he would go to these lengths to show reverence for the occasion. He's a good man and a good friend.

Your beauty should not come from outward adornment.... Instead, it should be that of your inner self, the unfading beauty of a gentle and quiet spirit, which is of great worth in God's sight.
                                                      —1 Peter 3:3–4

I like when we show proper respect with proper clothes, but as these verses clearly show, God lets us off the hook when we don't. He looks past the clothes and into the heart and mind and spirit, where others just can't see. If I had my choice, I'd choose a right heart over a right shirt any day. But in all honesty, I'd rather have both. Thanks be to God for all of us who do.

Stay dressed for action and keep your lamps burning.
                                                      —Luke 12:35

The Letter

A great custom of passing the power of office between presidents of the United States continues with each outgoing commander in chief to the next comes in the form of a handwritten letter. These letters are usually left in a drawer in the Oval Office and carry a personal message of congratulations and duty to the person who is about to take the seat behind that large, stately desk where only forty-six Americans have sat. (Actually forty-five, because Grover Cleveland is always counted twice.)

Don't know if you have ever thought about just how old this practice is, but I was curious enough to wonder if Washington had done it for Adams, if Buchanan had done it for Lincoln, Roosevelt for Taft, and so on and so forth. And I discovered that the tradition is not nearly as old as one would think. It started in modern-day history when President Reagan left the first note for George H. W. Bush on his Inauguration Day, January 20, 1989. It was a warm and friendly letter, clearly showing the unique and famous humor of Ronald Reagan. He had written the short note on a sheet of cartoon stationery that carried a sketch of an elephant lying down with turkeys crawling all over his back. The heading said, "Don't let the turkeys get you down."

Don Reid

The Bush letter to Clinton, four years later, included a very heartfelt sentiment crossing party lines: "Your success now is our country's success. I am rooting hard for you."

Clinton to George W. Bush, "My prayers are with you and your family. Godspeed."

Bush to Obama, "The critics will rage. Your 'friends' will disappoint you. But you will have an Almighty God to comfort you."

Obama to Trump, "Take time, in the rush of events and responsibilities, for friends and family. They'll get you through the inevitable rough patches. Good luck and God-speed."

There was a letter from Donald Trump to Joe Biden, but we have not yet been made privy to what it said. Maybe in time we will know and can add a sentence of encouragement to this list.

In thinking of these messages, my mind went directly to the Bible and all the writings that we think of as books but which are, in reality, long letters. The common belief is that of the twenty-seven books of the New Testament, twenty-one of them were letters in their original form. Our old friend Paul is accredited with at least thirteen epistles (letters) and maybe fourteen. (Some still argue today he might have written the book of Hebrews.)

So, how about Jesus? Did he ever write anything? The clear and safe answer is no. The only account of him physically writing is in John 8 when a woman, caught in adultery, was brought before him by the Pharisees to be judged. We're told he bent down and started to write on the ground with his finger. Not on parchment. Not with a quill. But with his finger in what was most probably sand. And as he was doing this he spoke:

If anyone of you is without sin, let him be the first to cast a stone at her.

—John 8:7

And then he went back to writing again on the ground. What he wrote that day is not known, but the words he spoke turned every one of those men slowly away, until no one was left but Jesus and the lone woman.

In his second letter to the Corinthians, Paul tops everything that has ever been put down on paper concerning letters, incoming or outgoing, for all generations.

Are we beginning to commend ourselves again? Or do we need, like some people, letters of recommendation to you or from you? You yourselves are our letter, written on our hearts, known and read by everybody. You show that you are a letter from Christ, the result of our ministry, written not with ink but with the spirit of the living God, not on tablets of stone but on tablets of human hearts.

—2 Corinthians 3:1–3

There is no nobler or more sacred role for us as Christians than to be a letter from Christ. It's a responsibility we will never live up to but will better ourselves every second of our lives by trying to. Keep the spirit in your heart and an eraser in your hand, and be the best possible letter you can be, signed humbly with love.

And don't let the turkeys get you down!

Remembering Dad

Have you ever spent any time walking through a cemetery reading the dates on the tombstones of family members? You'll become aware of that grandfather who lived in a period of history that you just never thought of before. Sure, the math adds up, but you somehow never realized he was around to see the things he saw. All of a sudden, it gives you a perspective on his life and his times you never had. Or maybe you'll find your grandmother was so much younger when she passed than you ever realized. Of course, you really don't have to go back even that far to be enlightened about your ancestors and the effect they may have had on your life.

Let's just look at Dad. Now if yours is still with you, you have the opportunity to talk to him about his times and experiences, but if, like me, he's not available to you any longer, those headstones can still offer some fantastic information. I walked that hilly graveyard just recently, and standing there counting the years on my fingers, I was given the revelation that my dad was thirty-seven years old when I was born. Then, tracing my own life back in time, I compared where I was at that age—mentally, spiritually, socially, responsibly, and maturely. By placing myself at the same age, I got an insight as to what he may have thought when he knew I was on the way. I got a hint of what he was feeling having another child at that age, taking on the obligations of a family of five instead of a family of four. Did he wonder if he could afford me? Did he wonder if he would have the time for me that he had had for my older brother and sister? Was he a little nervous about it all? Apprehensive? Afraid? What went on in his head and in his heart? Well, of course, I'll never know, but it gives me a new viewpoint and a new way of looking at his life and mine.

My dad taught me lots of things that have stuck with me through all these years. He taught me how to drive. Seems like that duty always falls to the man of the house. He taught me how to parallel park and how to check the oil and how to change it, and he made me buy my first car with my own money. But enough about me. (Right here, list a few things your dad taught you. And I realize everyone may not have had the luxury of having a dad in the house as they grew up, and for that I am so sincerely sorry.)

He taught me how to shoot a shotgun. How to sight it with one eye closed and how to hold it tight against my shoulder so the kick of it wouldn't knock me to the ground.

He instilled tithing in me. I remember him telling me more than once, "The more you give, the more you'll receive in so many different ways." He knew that feeling of helping someone in need and the rewards of the heart that stayed with you forever. (Again, right here add to your list another lesson you still cherish from your dad.)

We watched TV together as I was growing up. He loved the westerns. I still never watch an old *Gunsmoke*, *Rawhide*, or *Maverick* without finding my breath catch a little when I realize this was a particular favorite episode of his. We shared so much there in front of that old black-and-white table-model Motorola television set. The laughter and the conversations during commercials, the snacks on metal TV trays, the missed bedtimes he never enforced. Just a preteen kid and his dad enjoying the simple pleasures of life that have become golden memories imbedded in my heart so many, many years later.

The perfect father in the Scriptures was the symbolic father of the prodigal son in Jesus' parable—God, the Father, for sure. Reading that one over and over always reveals something new and comforting to me. We never had a fatted calf to kill or rings and robes to pass down, but I felt the devotion of a simple flesh-and-blood, right-out-of-the-fifties father who could not have served me better or loved me more.

Yeah, I walked that hilly graveyard this past week and stopped and visited for a few minutes. I told him I was going to write this and share some personal moments. He was okay with that.

Happy Father's Day.

Waking Tabitha

Dorcas or Tabitha? Call her by whichever name you choose. Either way, her story is the same and she's the same person.

Dorcas was her Greek name and Tabitha her Aramaic name. Let's just call her Tabitha for the sake of clarity. She lived in a town called Joppa there on the coast of the Mediterranean Sea. It's where Tel Aviv is today. Tabitha was a good woman of God, a charitable woman who made clothing for the needy. She was known all about the town for her good works and her acts of love for the poor. Everybody loved Tabitha, and when she fell sick and died, the people of Joppa were distraught.

Meanwhile, Peter was visiting in the neighboring town of Lydda, about fourteen miles inland of Joppa. A man there named Aeneas, who was paralyzed, had been bedridden for eight years. Peter said to this man, "Aeneas, Jesus Christ heals you. Get up and take your bed with you." Aeneas did, and the Scriptures tell us everyone who saw this miracle turned to the Lord.

Well, word of what Jesus had done through Peter traveled quickly, and when the people of Joppa got the news, they sent two men to find this miracle performer and ask him to please come to their town. When Peter and the two arrived, he was taken to Tabitha's house and upstairs to the room where her corpse lay. Gathered around her lifeless body was a group of widows, crying and mourning the loss of their treasured friend. The widows began to show Peter all the pretty robes and articles of clothing Tabitha had made by hand. But Peter's reaction was all business. He asked the women to leave the room. Then he got down on his knees and prayed. Turning to the deceased woman on the bed, he said, "Tabitha, get up!"

She opened her eyes, looked at Peter, and sat upright immediately! He took her by the hand and helped her to her feet. Then Peter called for the widows to come back in, along with many of the other saints and believers who were there.

All miracles are from God, but with this instance, Peter became only one of five people in all history to raise an individual from the dead. Thus, again we see the power and importance given Peter thanks to his extraordinary faith, love, and devotion.

Now if you are looking for some substantive Scripture on Peter that just might challenge your way of thinking, your politics, your lifestyle in general, I'm going to call your attention to a most interesting couple called Ananias and Sapphira. I love Scripture that makes me think and even squirm a little, and this passage certainly does that.

All the believers were one in heart and mind. No one claimed that any of their possessions was their own, but they shared everything they had. With great power the apostles continued to testify to the resurrection of the Lord Jesus. And God's grace was so powerfully at work in them all that there were no needy persons among them. For from time to time those who owned land or houses, sold them, brought the money from the sales and put it at the apostles' feet, and it was distributed to anyone who had need.

—Acts 4:32–35

Ananias and his wife, Sapphira, sold a piece of property. With his wife's full knowledge, Ananias kept back a little hunk of the money for himself. The rest he brought to the apostles and laid it at their feet. Peter, apparently being able to look into this man's heart, said, "Ananias, why have you lied to the Holy Spirit and kept back some of the money for yourself that you got from the sale of your land? What made you think of doing such a thing? You have not lied to men but you have lied to God."

Ananias, hearing these words, was so filled with fear and shame that he fell down and died at Peter's feet. Young men came, wrapped up his body, carried him away, and buried him.

Three hours later, Sapphira, his wife, came in, not knowing anything that had just happened. Peter asked her, "Tell me, is this the price you and Ananias got for the land?"

"Yes," she answered. "That is the price."

Peter looked at her earnestly and said, "How could you agree to test the spirit of the Lord? The feet of the men who buried your husband are at the door and they will carry you out also."

At that very moment, Sapphira fell at Peter's feet and died. The same young men carried her out and buried her beside her husband. The passage ends with:

Great fear seized the whole church and all who heard about these events.

—Acts 5:1–11

Don Reid

These are some of the things of the Bible we must study and ponder in our own personal moments, always seeking the guidance and understanding that God reveals to us in his own precious time. Honesty and integrity are cherished virtues in God's sight.

QUESTION FOR THOUGHT

Who were the other four people in the Bible besides Peter who raised an individual from the dead?

ANSWER

Elijah, Elisha, Jesus, and Paul. This may be the most exclusive club in the history of the world. To read these accounts, see:

1 Kings 17	Elijah
2 Kings 4	Elisha
2 Kings 13	Elisha
Luke 7	Jesus
Luke 8	Jesus
John 11	Jesus
Acts 9	Peter
Acts 20	Paul

Where's the Humor?

A collection of sixty-six books, and there is not one humorous story in there to entertain us between all the wars and desolation? How do you expect a person to wade through all that and not need a laugh somewhere along the way? And trust me, I've heard people make this point about the Bible. They want comic relief right along with the inspiration and sanctity. Of course, the distractors also like to say there is no place in all the books of Scripture that says Jesus ever smiled or laughed. And that is true. Probably true because we never gave him much reason to smile or laugh. And still don't today. But these shallow interpretations of the Bible hold no credence and carry no weight. And those who like to taunt believers with such pettiness are to be taken lightly, *like the chaff which the wind driveth away* (Ps. 1:4).

There's an Old Testament story that always brings a smile to my face. It is so descriptive that I can see it come alive in front of my eyes, and I laugh to myself every time I read it. It's the story of Elijah. He was kind of a wild man who sort of popped up out of nowhere over in the book of 1 Kings. He hid out in a ravine, at God's command, and drank his water from a brook and was fed bread and meat twice a day by the ravens. He performed miracles, including raising a boy back from the dead. But the one I'm getting to is the challenge he made to King Ahab, who was a Baal worshiper. Elijah faced off with 450 prophets of Baal to see who could call down fire—God or Baal.

The prophets went first. From early morning to noon, they prayed and chanted and cried and jumped and yelled for Baal to hear them, but to no avail. No fire. They pleaded and begged for the rest of the day, "Answer us, please, Baal!" But Baal just couldn't seem to hear them.

At this conjuncture of the game, Elijah showed a rare and sarcastic sense of humor. He began to tease them and say, "Shout louder. Maybe Baal can't hear you. Maybe he's busy or gone on a trip. Or maybe he's asleep. Holler louder!"

Elijah was making a point for the Lord and having fun doing it. The rest of the story, of course, was the Baal prophets continued until they could continue no more, and then Elijah took his turn. He had them douse the dry firewood with twelve barrels of water, and then stepped back and said, "God, let them know that you are God." And fire shot down from heaven while people fell on their faces and shouted, "The Lord is God!"

And Elijah wasn't through with the humor. He told King Ahab that even though there had been a drought for the past three years, the rains were about to commence. Elijah said, "You better get something to eat and drink and get out of here fast because the rain is coming."

The king ignored his advice, but as black clouds began to roll in, Elijah told him one more time, "Get in your chariot and get out of here. The rain is coming hard."

At this final warning, King Ahab jumped in his chariot and raced for shelter. Elijah took his coat off, stuffed it in his belt, and ran...are you ready for this? Ran *ahead* of the chariot all the way back to town! Now tell me that was not a funny sight, with old Elijah at full gallop outrunning those horses in the rain.

Jesus himself was not above a wink and a smile when it came to dealing with human beings. I call your attention to the story of the feeding of the five thousand (John 6). Jesus immediately sees the problem of feeding all those folks, and the Scriptures clearly tell us he already had in mind how he was going to handle it. That, however, did not keep him from testing one of them as to what he thought they should do. I just know he had a smile on his face when he asked Philip, "Where are we going to buy enough bread for all these people to eat?"

And that smile just got bigger when Philip came back with, "Eight months worth of wages wouldn't buy enough bread for everyone here to have a bite." (That answer could easily have been Philip's contribution to exaggeration humor.)

There is wit in words and in situations in our Bible if we just look for it and are open to it. Some of my childhood musical heroes in Southern gospel music were Hovie Lister and the Statesmen Quartet. Hovie, whom we got to know in later years, was a Southern Baptist minister but also a consummate pianist, singer, showman, and an energetic and funny storyteller. He could entertain you for hours either on the stage or on a backstage chair. Hovie was fond of saying, "The Lord never meant for religion to wear a long face."

I have to agree. There is no reason not to have fun if you're happy. And Christianity will surely make you happy!

A happy heart makes a cheerful face.
—Proverbs 15:13

After Christmas

Well, now the Christmas season is over. Everything you looked forward to and planned is behind you. Everything you dreaded and worried about is in the past. There may be mixed feelings in your household and in your heart. You may easily be conflicted about exactly what you're feeling at this moment. Look below and choose a word, or two or three, that fits what you're feeling so shortly after Christmas:

Relieved	Happy	Sorry	Glad
Tired	Relaxed	Melancholy	Peaceful
Restless	Fulfilled	Empty	Thankful
Sad	Reflective	Uplifted	Letdown
Spiritual	Satisfied		

Each choice here is very personal and each choice is a possibility for every one of us for different reasons. Sometimes it just helps to say it out loud.

The same applies to your tree and other Christmas decorations. Some of us may take them down the day after Christmas, some the week after Christmas, and others will do it after New Year's. There is no law of normalcy for these feelings either. Just whatever suits your vision and comfort in your respective celebration of the holy Christmas season.

Luke gives us a nice transition from the Christmas story to normal everyday living. He tells us what came next after the birth for Mary and Joseph and their newborn. All Jewish males are circumcised eight days after birth. This is called a Brit Milah, and it is performed by a "mohel." It is not a surgical procedure but a religious one. It can happen in a synagogue or in a home. The mohel is not a medical person but is experienced in this particular historic duty. Sometimes even the father of the child will perform it, but never the mother. (Although there is one case in the Old Testament of a mother rendering this duty. Zipporah, Moses' wife, circumcised her son with a sharp rock. But that, thank goodness, did not become the common way of getting this done.)

At this point, it's a good time for the question to come up as to why it had to be done at all. Well, it was Jewish law, and that was the world and culture Jesus was born into. It was a covenant made between God and Abraham two thousand years before Christ was even born, and it was a mark carried by males to show their relationship with God. It is still a practiced ceremony for Jews today. A "sandek" holds the baby on his lap while the mohel performs his duty. A third chair is placed beside them during this ceremony that is always empty. This chair is for the prophet Elijah, who attends every Brit Milah to protect the baby from danger. In many synagogues there is a permanent "Chair of Elijah." To assure that it is never sat in accidently by anyone, they hang it high on a ceremonial wall.

Luke also tells us that Jesus was officially named eight days after birth according to Old Testament law. The angel who appeared to Mary and Joseph before the birth had told them what his name was to be, but this made it official. And that is what was going on in the lives of Jesus and his parents immediately after the first Christmas.

There are a number of adjectives I didn't offer for what we may be feeling during this "after the holiday" period. I know the secular season can leave us drained and spent, but I sincerely hope the spiritual season has left us refreshed and renewed. There's something about the magic and the reverence of that Christmas Bible story that just never gets worn and tired, no matter how many times we read it or hear it or see it performed by little children in bathrobes and sandals. I hope everyone will carry a little piece of it into whatever new adventures in life you may take on in the coming days. Just a little bit of that wonderful old story will carry you a long way into whatever you undertake. Let this sweet old hymn be our theme for the coming days of that glorious new year.

> *Little is much when God is in it*
> *Labor not for wealth or fame*
> *There's a crown and you can win it*
> *If you go in Jesus' name*
>
> "Little Is Much"
> —Kittie Suffield

I Don't Know How to Pray

I've heard people make this statement, "I don't know how to pray," and it is usually from someone who wasn't raised in church or in a prayer-friendly family. And to be blatantly honest, I can understand something that is not practiced making a person feel awkward and uncomfortable. Anything new that we are introduced to has to get in our systems and become a part of who we are before we're easy and relaxed with it. If you've never dribbled a basketball, you just might not do it effectively the first time. If you've never ridden a bicycle, you might fall over and get skinned up a few times before you get it right. And you might remember how difficult it was keeping your daddy's Chevrolet between the lines on that first trip out on a real, live, four-lane highway. Putting a prayer together is only different in as much as it is easier than any of these other things, and we have definite instructions on how it's done, right there in the good old New Testament.

This is Jesus speaking in Matthew 6:7–13 and telling us exactly how it should be done:

When you pray, do not keep babbling on like pagans, for they think they will be heard for their many words.

Shakespeare said, "Brevity is the soul of wit." Jesus is telling us here it is the soul of so much more than that. It is a practice we should adhere to when speaking, even to God.

This, then, is how you should pray:

Address God and remember you are not praying to anyone else but him. Not even to Jesus. *Through* Jesus, but not *to* him. Jesus never told us to pray to anyone but the Father.

Our Father, which art in heaven.

Then give him praise so you will know and be aware of in your heart just exactly to whom you are speaking.

Hallowed be thy name. Thy kingdom come. Thy will be done in earth, as it is in heaven.

Next, petition him and request what will fulfill your present needs.

Give us this day our daily bread. And forgive us our debts as we forgive our debtors. And lead us not into temptation, but deliver us from evil.

As we near the end of a prayer, recognize him again and give him glory.

For thine is the kingdom, and the power, and the glory, forever, Amen.

Some people develop the beautiful knack of praying so fluidly and so gracefully that it's as if the words are just falling from their lips onto the ear of God. And while others may falter and stumble through their sentences, I don't think God ever hears the difference. It is the heart he's listening to and communicating and connecting with. But hearing one who is practiced in the art of prayer is a pleasing comfort to us mortals.

It was always a custom for The Statlers to have a prayer every night before a performance. The four of us would form a circle in the aisle of our tour bus or in a dressing room backstage and take turns, from night to night, having the prayer. On occasions, we were joined by friends and other entertainers on the show. I won't drop names of all who have been in that circle with us, but I will tell you of one of the most memorable. It was during the seven years of our Saturday night TV series. We were about to go on the air but had stopped off in a room by the studio stage to have our prayer. One of the guests on the show that night was Vestal Goodman of the Happy Goodman Family. She was the Queen of Southern Gospel Music. Sweet Vestal with the high hair and the most powerful and perfect voice God ever put in a human body. I asked her if she would like to join us, and as the five of us stood there in that small room, I invited her to pray.

You know how certain things send a quick chill up your spine? Well, from the moment she began until she got to "Amen," I almost froze to death!

This lady talked to God as if we were sitting across the table from him with coffee cups in front of us. With her eyes tightly clinched and her hands raised, the longer she talked, the weaker I got in the knees. Everyone was feeling it. When she finished, we all had tears in our eyes and there was a thin skim of ice on my back. I just grabbed her and hugged her. God was so surely in that room that night, and we were never more motived to hit the air than we were at that very moment.

The lesson to be learned by us all is that a true and good prayer is just a true and good conversation with the Lord. He's there to listen and receive like a close friend who hears your problems without judgement. He doesn't expect all of us to be as adept as Vestal, and thank heavens we don't have to be, because he hears what we feel and sees what we think.

Don't know how to pray? Quit overthinking it. Treat it like anything else in life and just do it. God will take care of the rest.

The Unpardonable Sin

Some stories we experience firsthand, while for others we have to depend on the veracity of strangers (to paraphrase Tennessee Williams). This little tale falls somewhere in between, as I was not there but was told about it by someone who was.

A minister was interviewing for the position of head pastor with a committee from the church congregation. After answering all their many questions about his theology, preaching methods, and character, he boldly said to them, "And here's something more you need to know about me. I smoke, I drink, and I cuss." The committee reconvened privately in one of the Sunday school rooms for a few minutes. When they came out, they shook hands with the minister and hired him.

There's a lot to be gleaned from this true story. Honesty is the best policy? Confession is good for the soul? This was the thirty-fifth preacher they had interviewed and wanted to get it over with? You can decide how it best speaks to you and exactly what it is saying.

What I see in it is that this small committee considered this man's admitted shortcomings and decided to forgive or just overlook these flaws until something bigger came along. Now, true, he never asked for any consideration or offered to make any changes in his lifestyle, but then so often those who do never get around to it anyway, so there you go. If these trans-gressions were sins on a larger scale, then this committee might have been overwhelmed and unable to make any kind of clear, immediate decision. If he had confessed to extortion or robbery or murder, then that kicks things up a notch or two. But even then, God promises us that if we are truly sorry and promise to do better, he will forgive and give us a clean heart. And that is an offer that no one can refuse (to paraphrase Don Corleone).

Then there is always someone sitting on the sideline just waiting to throw a fish in the drinking water and say, "But what about that one unpardonable sin that even God says he won't forgive?" Yeah, what about that one? So much has been misun-derstood about it down through the years that there are legends and falsehoods about what it exactly means. To get one big and serious obstacle off the table, it is not suicide. That theory will come up every time the topic does, but it is just a folktale of misinformation.

The true definition of the sin that God won't forgive comes from Jesus himself, and here's the scene. The Pharisees and the lawyers proclaimed that the miracles Jesus performed were coming from Satan. They were professing that Jesus had an evil spirit about him. And this is how he answered that ac-cusation:

> *And so I tell you, every sin and blasphemy will be for-given men, but the blasphemy against the Spirit will not be forgiven. Anyone who speaks a word against the Son of Man will be forgiven, but anyone who speaks against the Holy Spirit will not be forgiven, either in this age or the age to come.*
>
> —Matthew 12:31–32

I tell you the truth, all sins and blasphemies of men will be forgiven them. But whosoever blasphemes against the Holy Spirit will never be forgiven; he is guilty of an eternal sin. He said this because they were saying, "He has an evil spirit."

—Mark 3:28–30

It seems odd that this concept has been so misunderstood by so many believers through the years when it really is very plainly stated in these two passages. If someone doesn't claim the work of the Lord to be the work of the devil, then they are safely under the grace and forgiveness of God. No matter what we have done and will do, if we believe and profess our belief in Christ, we're covered. We are not perfect and that is no surprise to God. He never thought we were. We can't shock him. We can't tell him something he hasn't heard. And we can't hide our true hearts from him, so don't even try. Just like that preacher who was being interviewed and who probably told more than he needed to about himself, we are an open book when we sit down to talk to and pray to God in private. And we can be as honest and as vulnerable with him as we are with the oldest and most trusted friend we have. Remember, God never made a man (or woman) he didn't love (to paraphrase Will Rogers).

For God so loved the world that he gave his only begotten Son, that whosoever believeth in him should not perish but have everlasting life.

—John 3:16

Opening Doors and Knocking Down Walls

And here is the Peter story of stories that is the most important to you and me. It is the story about the responsibility he was given that would give non-Jewish folk, like us, the path to heaven.

Cornelius was a Roman centurion stationed with his family in the town of Caesarea. They were God-fearing people who gave generously to those in need and prayed devoutly. One day, at three o'clock in the afternoon, Cornelius had a vision. An angel came to him and said, "Cornelius, your prayers and your charity have come up as a memorial offering before God. Send some men to Joppa and bring back one known as Peter. He is staying at the home of a man named Simon the tanner, whose house is by the sea."

As soon as the angel left, Cornelius called in two servants and a soldier he trusted and sent them thirty miles due south to Joppa to bring to him this man called Peter. (If you remember, Peter had been in the town of Lydda when two men from Joppa came and told him he was needed there. Now three men are sent to Joppa from Caesarea to tell him he's needed there.) And keep in mind Cornelius was doing all this on faith, as the angel never gave him any reason for these instructions.

About noon the following day, not knowing men were on their way to find him, Peter went up on the roof of the house where he was staying to pray. While there, he got hungry, and as his meal was being prepared, he fell into a trance. Heaven opened up to him and a large sheet came down containing all kinds of four-footed animals, wild beasts, reptiles, and birds.

Then a voice said, "Get up, Peter. Kill and eat!"

Peter said, "But Lord, I have never eaten anything impure and unclean."

The voice came back at him with, "Do not call anything impure that God has made clean."

This whole scenario was played out three times (things happening three times seems to be a pattern in Peter's life), and then the sheet just ascended back to where it came from. While Peter sat scratching his head over what had just happened to him, the three messengers stood downstairs at the door and called in, "Is there a man named Peter staying here?" (Note they did not enter the house, as strict Jews did not let Gentiles into their homes, nor did Jews go into Gentiles' homes.)

Before Peter could react, the voice of the Holy Spirit spoke again and said, "These men are looking for you. Go downstairs and do not hesitate to go with them for I have sent them here."

The three men stood at the door and told Peter they were here at the request of Cornelius the centurion, a righteous man who had been told by a holy angel to have him come to his home so he could hear what Peter had to say. And this is a pivotal moment in the history of our salvation, because at this instant Peter opened the door to these three men and opened the door to heaven to *all* who believe, no matter their heritage.

The next day, the three envoys, three townsmen from Joppa, and Peter set out for Caesarea. When Peter came to the door of the Roman's home, no doubt Cornelius had to wonder if he would indeed cross the threshold; but Peter never faltered and walked through the doorway. The barriers were beginning to go down. Cornelius fell at his feet, but Peter said, "Stand up. I am only a man myself. God has shown me I shall not call any man impure or unclean. I now realize that God does not show favoritism."

And then he preached to the family of Cornelius who had gathered in his house. And the Holy Spirit came on *all* who heard his message, both Jew and Gentile, both circumcised and uncircumcised. God had offered salvation to all believers and had cleansed food that had been forbidden under Jewish law.

Peter got a lot of heat from the Jewish believers and was criticized for consorting with those unclean Gentiles. But our man stood his ground and said back to them, "If God gave them the same gift he gave us, who was I to think that I could oppose God?"

When his dissenters heard this, they offered no further argument or objections.

And all God's people say, "Amen."

QUESTION FOR THOUGHT

Why was it unusual that Peter was staying in the home of Simon the tanner in Joppa?

ANSWER

The mere fact that he was a tanner tells us he was a Gentile. By Jewish law, Jews deemed the handling of dead animals unclean. So, Peter staying as a guest in this home was already the beginning of opening doors and knocking down the walls between the Jews and the Gentiles, even before the heavenly drama on Simon's roof.

Epiphany Sunday

Happy New Year!

It is only befitting we give a little attention to the day of Epiphany on January 6. The word is very interesting in the different ways it's often used. Uncapitalized, it means, of course, an appearance; a manifestation; a discovery. But capitalized, the church recognizes it as the arrival of the wise men to Bethlehem and commemorates their visit to the newborn Son of God. There is so much written in various history books about them but so very little written in our Bible that it's hard to say much about them and still be true to Scripture.

Those who have expanded on the facts found in the New Testament have often come under a great deal of scrutiny. Let's take, for example, one of our more famous Christmas carols, "We Three Kings."

The opening line is *We three kings*. Well, the Bible never says if there were three or twelve or thirty-seven. Any number put to their grouping is speculation and not factual. Matthew does tell us they brought three gifts, so that is probably where the number three was born and then perpetuated down through the years.

That same opening line of *We three kings* has a double whammy of imperfection. The Bible never says they were kings. You may find in your preferred translation they are called Magi, meaning magicians or astrologers, but wait a minute: the King James Version, the first and earliest of the English translations, doesn't even use that word. It simply says "wise men" and uncapitalized at that. Not a title but just men who were wise.

This song was written in 1857, and even though it has garnered a great deal of popularity, it is not a well-respected piece of music by those in authority. Many hymnbooks have excluded it. Hymnologists, those who choose songs for hymnals, have often refused to include it in their publications because it is just not factual according to Scripture. And with all that said, here is the real kicker. It was written, words and music, by Henry Hopkins Jr., an Episcopal minister from Vermont.

I don't want it to sound like I am disparaging or belittling the Reverend Hopkins in any way, because that is not my intention. As a matter of fact, I have to admit that getting past the title and the first line, I rather admire him as a songwriter. His second verse is about the gift of gold. His third about the frankincense. And his fourth verse is myrrh. Very clever and well done. But the best is left for the fifth and last verse as he clearly writes about Easter!

Glorious now behold Him arise
King and God and Sacrifice
Alleluia, Alleluia
Sounds thro' the earth and skies

This day of Epiphany is the official ending of the Christmas season. There will be no more mention of Christmas in the church calendar until December. All the

decorations are gone. All the color is gone. The baby Jesus
story has been put to bed for another season, and now it's the
study again of the adult Jesus and his teachings. We all have
to grow up a little after each Christmas and get back to the
reality of our lives and our Christian responsibilities. The
trees, the gifting, the Christmas programs, and the carols are
all tucked away until another year. And I, for one, am sorry
to see it go. But as we do, let me ask you one heartfelt question. Of all the things you did this past season, what was the
one important moment that truly made it Christmas for you?

I wish we were all together to hear everyone's answer.
But think about it seriously and sometime this week share
your answer with someone you love.

> *And when they were come into the house, they saw the
> young child with Mary his mother, and fell down and
> worshipped him.*

> —Matthew 2:11

Your Best Friend

So much has been written about friendship in poems, prose, and songs. The reason for that is because it is so important to us on a daily basis. We all need friends in our lives. We need camaraderie. We need comfortable relationships. I believe you can die from loneliness, and I believe too many sad folks do every day. I'll just be one of millions who have taken a stab in verse and text to define what friendship means. Here's my take. Please add to it to suit your heart.

A friend is:

1. Someone you can be totally honest with.
2. Someone you can trust to keep a secret.
3. Someone who won't judge every mistake you make.
4. Someone who won't believe a lie about you.
5. Someone who will tell you the truth no matter how much it may hurt.
6. Someone who will tolerate your moods.
7. Someone who will overlook your little annoyances.
8. Someone who will say something good about you behind your back.
9. Someone you don't have to constantly prove yourself to.
10. Someone who still loves you when you're not being likeable.

A great example of friendship can be lifted right out of the Scriptures in the persons of David and Jonathan. Everyone knows of their loyalty to one another, but there is a wonderful, often overlooked story over in the book of 2 Samuel that surpasses anything we know of love and loyalty to a friend.

When King Saul and son Jonathan died together in battle, Jonathan's son, Mephibosheth, was only five years old. Hearing the news and being afraid for their lives, his nurse grabbed the boy up to flee the country. In doing so, she dropped him or he fell and injured his legs, and he was crippled for the rest of his life.

Flash ahead many years later. David is now the king, and he is remembering an instance in their lives when Jonathan had asked him to never cut off his kindness from his family. It was as if Jonathan saw into the future and knew David would someday rise to become king. It was not unheard of for a new king to kill the family of the previous reign if there was any hostility at all, and there were certainly some hard feelings between Saul and David. But these two men had a pact, and David promised never to cut off his kindness from Jonathan's descendants. To show the kind of man and king he was, years after Saul and Jonathan were dead, David asked Ziba, an old servant of Saul's, if there was anyone left of the family to whom he could show some kindness.

Old Ziba scratched his head and thought and finally said, "Yeah, there is still a grandson of Saul's somewhere. A son of Jonathan's actually. He's crippled in both feet. Can't walk at all."

"Bring him to me," David said.

So, Mephibosheth was delivered to the king, and he bowed down before him, as everyone did. But David said to him, "Don't be afraid. I didn't bring you here to harm you. I'm fulfilling a promise I made your father, Jonathan, who was my best friend. I'm going to give you all the land and all the possessions that belonged to your grandfather, King Saul, and you will always eat at my table."

Then David called Ziba in again and said to him, "I've given Mephibosheth all of his family's land, and from now on I want you and your fifteen sons to farm that land for him and take care of him, as he is in no physical condition to provide for himself."

And from that day on, Mephibosheth, son of David's best friend, came and lived in Jerusalem and ate daily at the king's table.

I want you, right now, to take paper and pen and write down the three best friends you have ever had in your life. Then I want you to write down the three best friends you have at this moment. (They change. Circumstances change. Life changes.) Next, I want you to call, text, or email them and tell them what they mean to you. They will appreciate the call more than you can imagine. And so will you.

And please tell them I say hello.

I Found It at the Bookstore

I've spent half my life walking the aisles and searching the shelves of bookstores in practically every city I have ever been in. Every continent, every country, every state, every city or county road with a new or used book sign hanging above the door, I've been in it. And I can spend hours just roaming in and out of the mystery section to the music section to the new fiction section to religious research...well, you get the picture. I just love books.

I feel a comfort being among books. I so like the touch and feel of leafing through them that I have never down-loaded a book online. It just wouldn't be the same. I like the weight in my hand, the numbered pages I can easily look back through for a missed fact, the way I can see how many pages I have before I finish, and just the whole production of the picture on the front and the little bio of the author on the inside flap. And as I think about all the stores I've spent so much time in over a lifetime, and all the books I've bought from them, I'm reminded of some stories that have stuck with me through the years.

It was many decades ago when I walked in the door of a mom-and-pop bookstore (something you sadly don't see much anymore) in a Midwestern city one spring morning. It was spring for sure because I remember distinctly the front door was propped open, which always makes for a friendly welcome. A very young clerk spoke to me from behind the counter and said, "Come on in! Can I help you?"

Even though I was prepared to browse and find things on my own, I said, "Sure. I'm looking for the new Billy Graham book called *Angels*. Do you have it in yet?"

"Yes, we surely do," he said as he came around the counter and headed to a nearby shelf. "And are you in luck! We just got a shipment of them in yesterday, and they are all flawed, so we have them on sale for half price."

A brand-new book at half price? "What's the flaw?" I asked him.

"Well," he said, "as I was unpacking them yesterday, I noticed every one of them was printed upside down. So, we will have to take a hit on them at half price."

I took the book, took the young man at his word, and when I left, I included *Angels* in the stack of books I bought and he bagged. A few days later, while traveling back across the country, I pulled out my satchel of books and inspected the situation a little closer and solved the mystery of the flawed printing. There was absolutely nothing wrong with the book. Apparently, the factory had just slipped the dust jacket covers on upside down and this poor young fellow had given away all his profits and maybe some of Billy Graham's. (And maybe that's why the big-box bookstores are all you can find today.)

Another city, another time, I found myself wandering into another bookshop with a few hours to kill. This happened to be a Christian bookstore, and I happened to be having little luck in finding a title I was looking for. I went to the counter and told the lady my dilemma, and she turned immediately to the computer. In short time, she said, "Yes, we have one copy left according to this screen, but let me look on the shelf to make sure we really do have it."

I sort of laughed as I followed her back through the store and said, "Well, if the computer says you have it but you don't have it on the shelf, that can only mean one thing. Somebody has stolen it."

She stopped abruptly, turned and looked at me over her glasses, and said, "That happens every day in here."

A little shocked, I said, "What! People shoplifting books in a Christian bookstore?"

She nodded emphatically and said, "You'd better believe it. They steal Bibles all the time."

Again, it was my turn to be stunned. "What kind of confused, conflicted person would it take to steal a Bible?"

"Ah, honey," she said, "people will steal anything that ain't nailed to the floor." And she was off to find the title I was in search of.

Just goes to prove you can find anything in a bookstore. And it isn't always something you can read. Sometimes it's something that keeps you scratching your head for years to come. Maybe that's part of the charm I have always enjoyed about these quiet, clean, cerebral places.

You never know what adventure or lesson might be around the corner of the next aisle.

What Are You Doing New Year's Eve?

Maybe it's much too early in the game
Ah, but I thought I'd ask you just the same
What are you doing New Year's, New Year's Eve?

That's a wonderful old pop song from 1947, first recorded by Margret Whiting and written by Broadway songsmith Frank Loesser. It is the only song I know of that is written specifically for New Year's Eve. There are few floating around out there to commemorate this particular holiday. And even fewer stories in the Bible to shed much light on the way we celebrate the beginning of our year, based mainly on the Roman calendar. But here is a verse from the Good Book I always find fits the need of Christians this time of the year:

> *Therefore, if anyone is in Christ, he is a new creation;*
> *the old has gone, the new has come.*
> —2 Corinthians 5:17

And that is basically what we still celebrate in our daily lives on New Year's Day. We throw out the old and rejoice in the new! So, however you may choose to spend New Year's Eve, whether with friends, dancing the night away, sitting in front of the TV watching the ball drop, enjoying a romantic dinner with the love of your life, or with family gathered around the dining room table, you may find my lit-tle concoction of conversational questions suitable for the occasion. All ages can play, so just throw them out there in the air, and I promise they will invoke attitudes and stories that will enlighten and entertain. Everybody, all together now, one, two, three...and here we go!

1. Give three words that best describe this past year for you.
2. Name one really good thing that happened to you this year.
3. What do you most look forward to in the year ahead?
4. What is the one thing you want to do next year that you didn't get to do this year?
5. Is there any particular lesson this past year taught you?
6. How would you like to spend more of your free time next year?
7. What is your dream vacation for some year in the future?
8. Name something nice someone did for you this past year.
9. Did you make a new friend this past year and who was it?
10. Did you make a resolution last New Year's Day you kept all year long?

We have a family tradition of eating dinner together every New Year's Eve—all the kids and the grandkids—and then we just sit around the table and talk and pass these questions out. We all come in our pajamas and stay till mid-night, playing games, laughing, and eating ourselves silly. Stories abound, memories are made, and when the night is over, we have learned a little bit more about each other than we knew when we started. We have watched the old pass out through the window and the new come in through the door. We are truly blessed.

> *God himself will be with them and be their God. He will wipe every tear from their eyes. There will be no more death or mourning or crying or pain, for the old order of things has passed away.*
> —Revelation 21:3–4

> *Ah, but in case I stand one little chance*
> *Here's the jackpot question in advance*
> *What are you doing New Year's, New Year's Eve?*
> "What Are You Doing New Year's Eve?"
> —Frank Loesser

Prison Break and Poof!

This is the twelfth and final chapter on the Apostle Peter. We have covered highlights in his life and his mission just enough to reacquaint ourselves with the importance this man possessed in first carrying the Word and then establishing the early church. This is the last singular heroic event in his biography that shows him to be the pillar we like to remember.

King Herod was arresting people who were associated with the church. He actually had the Apostle James executed by sword. When he saw how this pleased the Jewish community, he stepped up his game and arrested another of James's kind, his cohort Peter. He threw him in prison with plans to bring him to trial after the Passover, with a certain death sentence to follow. In prison, Peter was under the heavy guard of four squads of four soldiers each. (Note: that would be sixteen guards watching this one man, in chains, around the clock.) Herod was taking no chances. But all this time, the church, in the privacy of homes, was praying for Peter, and what was about to happen was a fantastic miracle that Herod could never have expected, dreamed of, or imagined in his wildest thoughts.

The night before his trial, Peter was sleeping in chains between two soldiers, with sentries standing in the doorways.

There was absolutely no way for anyone to get in or out of his cell, when a sudden light came on and an angel appeared and tapped Peter on the shoulder. "Quick. Get up," he said, and the chains just fell off Peter's wrists. "Put on your clothes, your shoes, and wrap your coat around yourself and follow me."

Peter, a little stunned by it all, did what he was told but had no clear idea of what was happening to him. He truly thought he was seeing a vision. Following the angel, they passed the first guards, and then the second guards, until they finally came to the iron gate that led out into the city. The gate, as if on its own strength, opened for them, and they simply walked through the entrance. They walked together for about a block when there, in the middle of the street, right in front of Peter's eyes, *poof,* the angel disappeared.

At this point, poor old Peter came to himself and was clear-headed and straight-thinking. He knew in his heart and mind what had just happened. An angel of God had just busted him out of prison but then had left him standing there alone in the night. It dawned on him his next move was to find someplace to hide. He immediately thought of the home of Mary, the mother of John Mark, where many of the Christians had gathered to pray for him. When they heard him knocking at the door and then saw him standing there, they were astonished but happily surprised. Peter shushed them, told them all what had just happened, and then quickly left for a secret place.

Herod's men searched high and low for him but to no avail. Peter was nowhere to be found. This inflamed the already wounded ego of the king, and giving in to the all-too-human need of having someone to blame, he had the prison guards arrested and executed.

A double ending to this amazing story was the demise of King Herod. Shortly after this escapade, while sitting on his throne in his royal robes, for all of his evilness and for his constant rejection of God, an angel of the Lord struck him down and he was eaten by worms and died. (Note: the Bible clearly says "eaten by worms and died," not "died and eaten by worms." Wow, sorry about that, Herod.)

At this point, Luke, the author of Acts, does a rather strange thing. He donates the first twelve chapters of his book to the life and times of Peter, but abruptly after this jailbreak, he switches his focus totally to Paul and never mentions Peter's name but once more in the next sixteen chapters. As a matter of fact, Peter is never mentioned in the Bible again until over in Galatians when he and Paul have that little vis-à-vis dustup about the Jews and the Gentiles. That short story is covered in about seven verses and then he disappears again until his two books, 1 Peter and 2 Peter. After this, we hear nothing about Jesus' right-hand man, the man who established the early Christian church, the man who tradition tells us asked to be crucified upside down because he was not worthy to die as Jesus had died.

We leave Peter, I hope, with a little better understanding of his strengths and weaknesses, his passions, his human frailties, his undying faith and love for Christ, and his special and uncontested place in the history of our church. I've enjoyed this closer look and renewed friendship with this man called Peter.

I leave this series with the last words Peter wrote in his final book in the Bible:

Grow in grace and in the knowledge of our Lord and Savior Jesus Christ, to him be glory both now and forever, Amen.

—2 Peter 3:18

QUESTION FOR THOUGHT

Which writer wrote the largest part of the New Testament: Paul, Luke, or John?

ANSWER

Luke.
John wrote five books with a word count of 28,091.
And Paul wrote thirteen books with a word count of 32,408.
But Luke, with just two books, contributed a word count of 37,932.

So, What Denomination Are You?

I am going to make an uneducated guess that at least half of everyone reading this right now who is a churchgoer has been a member of more than one denomination. It has been my experience that folks don't just change churches from time to time, but in the process, flip over to other theologies and spiritual ways of thinking at different points of their lives. Maybe you've investigated the doctrines and decided that you like the way they do things across the street at the Episcopal church. You like the liturgies and the rites and the more formal ways of worship. And if this suits your nature and you find it more inspiring, I think that is just fine.

Or it could be you find yourself more in tune with the Lutherans down the pike. You prefer their thinking in the presenting of the Lord's Supper. It's called consubstantiation, meaning they believe the body of Christ is "in, with, and under" the bread. They also have a tiered form of government with bishops as key officials. And if this is more appealing to you, then I think that is just fine.

Could be, on the other hand, you find you have a leaning toward that pretty, stately, old Methodist church on the corner downtown. You feel John Wesley had the right ideas in order when he put this denomination in motion. You like their take on social issues and their belief in the human decision in one's conversion. And you want your minister to stay on the move about every five years. If this makes you more comfortable and in closer touch with the Holy Spirit, I think that, too, is just fine.

And if that Baptist church out there in the county or across town, and there are many different brands (Southern, American, Primitive, National, Reformed, etc.), catches your eye, you just may want to give *it* a try. You may like the sound of "free will" instead of "predestination." You may feel more cleansed with "full immersion" than "a sprinkling" when it comes to baptism. And if all this gives you a warmer feeling of the presence of God, then I think this is absolutely just fine. As long as Jesus is in them all, everything will be okay.

I still belong to the very same denomination I was born into. Even go to the very same church into which I was born, reared, baptized, and joined at the early age of twelve. So, what could I possibly add to this discussion? More than you might think, as I have a story I feel compelled to tell on myself at this particular point.

Debbie is Southern Baptist while I am Presbyterian. We never saw a need to change that situation when we married, and we are very happy with the arrangement to this day. I go to many of her events, and she goes to many of mine, but we both head different ways on Sunday mornings. This story, however, begins on a Wednesday night in a Bible study at her Baptist church quite a few years ago. I love all her fellow members and always feel at home there, and especially at these informal, roundtable discussions in the middle of the week.

One night, the topic of denominations came up, and knowing that I was the only non-Baptist in the room, someone, more out of fun than challenge, said, "Hey, Don. Why are you a Presbyterian?"

I had to smile at this as I had never been pointedly asked such a question, but I took great pride in giving what I thought was a very profound answer. I took off on an in-depth, oral dissertation about John Calvin and John Knox and their tenets of the faith and some of that glorious stuff about predestination and the elect and just all kinds of sixteenth-century Scottish theology. Aw, man! Was I ever impressive!

But then the next day, I got to thinking about what all I had said, and I went over to see my mother. I asked her, "Mom, why are we Presbyterians?"

She said, in her gentle and matter-of-fact way, "Well, your grandfather [that would have been *her* father] was born and raised a Lutheran. And he is the one who made the change."

By this time, I'm thinking to myself, "Really?" I had never heard this story before. My grandfather was deeper into all this than I had ever given him credit for. It was my turn to be impressed. I said to her, "You're telling me he's the one who changed the family's whole denomination?"

She said, "Yes, he was. When he married your grandmother and they set up housekeeping and got a home of their own...their house was closer to the Presbyterian church than it was to the Lutheran church. And that is why you're a Presbyterian!"

My dear mother could always bring things down to an earthly understanding and leave me, though a little deflated, always laughing at myself. Did I go back to that Baptist Bible study group and correct what I had told them? No, I did not. I'll let them read it right here the same way you did.

And I'm still laughing at myself!

Who Do You Trust?

Back in the Dark Ages, when I was a kid, there was a day-time television show every afternoon called "Who Do You Trust?" The host, a very young Johnny Carson, would give a married couple a topic such as music, or sports, or history, and they would have to decide which one of them they would trust to correctly answer a question about this subject. For instance, for music, the man might say, "My wife will know more about this than I do." Then Johnny would ask her, "What instrument does Louie Armstrong play?" The wife would answer "Trumpet," and points would go on the board for them. They would play against another couple standing on the stage. Pretty mild stuff, but it showed a truth and trust between two married people and how well they knew one another. It would make for a good family board game even today, and maybe there is one for all I know. (Of course, to-day no one would know who Louie Armstrong was, so you'd have to change it to "What instrument does John Legend play?")

Brother Harold and I used to play a game of trust when we were kids and even as teenagers and young men. It started out as a parlor stunt and then grew to become more public as we saw the effect it had on people. They never failed to gasp and put their hands to their faces. And the more shocked they were, the more often we did it. While standing around talking in a group of people, I would, with no warning at all, just put my feet together and my hands straight down my sides, stiffen myself, and say, "Here I come!" Then I would fall backward, and he would cup his hands and catch my head just before I hit the hardwood floor or the concrete sidewalk, depending on where we were moved to put on this little exposition. Trust me, it takes trust. I don't advise anyone to go out and try this because it takes 100 percent confidence in the person doing the catching.

I was riding down a busy highway not long ago and passed a woman on a bicycle reading a book. Yes, I promise you this is true. She had an attachment on her handlebars with clips to keep the pages from flapping in the wind, and she was reading and riding. Now I don't have this kind of trust, because this poor misguided young lady was trusting that everyone on the road was going to be looking out for her. Understand, I have faith, but I don't have that kind of trust in my fellow man, and especially when they're behind the wheel.

The classic story of trust is over in the book of Acts, chapter nine. Jesus had just struck Saul blind on the road to Damascus while making him see the light. He led him into town, and for three days he couldn't see and didn't eat or drink anything. Living there in Damascus was a very faithful disciple to whom Jesus came to visit in a vision.

"Ananias!"

"Yes, Lord."

"Go to the house of Judas on Straight Street and ask for a man named Saul from Tarsus. He is praying right now but he has had a vision that a man named Ananias will come and place his hands on him and restore his sight."

Ananias was reluctant and said, "Lord, I have heard about this man. I know all about him. I know all the harm he has done to your followers in Jerusalem. He has come here with authority from the chief priests to arrest anyone who believes in you and calls on your name."

But the Lord said to Ananias, "Go! This man is my chosen instrument to carry my name to the Gentiles and to the people of Israel."

Showing total and unreserved trust, Ananias got up and went to the house on Straight Street, laid his hands on Saul, and said, "Brother Saul, Jesus, who appeared to you on the road sent me here so that you may see again."

At this, scales fell from his eyes and he could see.

That is the true meaning of trust. To know that God is right even when we have proof before us that our thoughts are correct with the facts, that what we are thinking is a better solution. Trust is never doubting. Never questioning. Never hesitating.

Looking back on that little trust stunt Harold and I pulled so often, I just realized we never switched roles. Could it be he didn't trust me as much as I trusted him, or was it that he was just smarter than I was?

Ah, the memories that flood my soul.

Your Favorite Teacher

Jesus was called "teacher" no less than sixty times in the Bible. It was an honorable title and the way his disciples looked upon him. They weren't always sure of their firm beliefs of him as their Savior until after the Resurrection, but they loved and respected him as their rabbi and educator.

You call me teacher and Lord and rightly so, for that is what I am.

—John 13:13

There are certain questions you can ask anyone that will produce good memories and answers that will boost any conversation lag that might exist. "What's your favorite song?" "Favorite movie?" "Favorite book?" "Who was your favorite teacher and why?" Off the top of my head, three different names come to mind on that last one, and I could do twenty minutes on each one of them.

Teachers form who we are. Good ones bring a fresh way of giving us new information, and the really good ones leave us with thoughts that never go away. They change not only our minds, but they change our hearts and our methods of doing and feeling. This story of a favorite teacher is not mine. I borrow it with all respect from my wife, Debbie. She told me this story early on in our lives together, and it gave me an insight into her and who she was. What people remember, and how they remember it, is a glimpse into their soul and tells so much about who they really are.

It was junior high in west Tennessee, in the little town of Milan. Debbie was twelve years old. She was given a homework assignment one night to read a number of pages in her science book. Science was a tough struggle for her at best (and one that I can certainly relate to). After supper that evening, she read the pages and then read them again. The second time was even more confusing than the first. The subject of the lesson was "infinity," and she just couldn't seem to grasp it.

Now, that's a mighty big subject for a twelve-year-old mind. It's a big subject for a mind of any age. She looked it up and the definition didn't really help much. Boundless. Endless. Unlimited. Wow! This called for some serious help, so she got on the phone and called two of her girlfriends who shared the same class. For once, they really were on the phone talking about homework and not boys. But what she learned was that they were just as confused as she was. None of the three could comprehend or explain this thing called infinity.

Worried that the teacher might pop a quiz on them the first thing the next day, they decided to go to school a few minutes earlier than normal and just level with her to see if she could make it clearer than the textbook had. So, early the next morning, these three young girls walked to school together and into Mrs. Mayo's room before anyone else had arrived for class, and stood in front of her desk. Mrs. Mayo was reading the newspaper, and as she sensed this trio standing there, she lowered the paper and said, "Good morning, ladies. Can I help you?"

They, all three at once, explained why they were there, and then simply asked, "Can you tell us in your own words, what is infinity?"

This beloved teacher of theirs, looked at those three sincere, youthful faces and smiled sweetly at each of them. She slowly folded the paper and put it on her desk, then took off her glasses and looked off somewhere over the top of their heads, and said, more to herself than to them, "Well, let's see. Infinity. Infinity is...

When we've been there ten thousand years
Bright shining as the sun
We've no less days to sing God's praise
Than when we first begun

"Amazing Grace"
—John Newton

God bless you, Mrs. Mayo, for everything you were. Today you might be fired for that answer.

A student is not above his teacher, but everyone who is
fully trained will be like his teacher.

—Luke 6:40

(Note: Lois Mayo died in December of 2020 at the age of 104. She was a lifetime inspiration to Debbie. And also to me, just from this one story, as I never met her. A life well lived is a memory never forgotten.)

In Summary—All About You

This book has been about *my* Life Lessons. I would never presume to be so wise to write advice to others, only to share what I have experienced. In the hope that someone may benefit from some of my words, I have opened my heart and so many of my memories in order to persuade and encourage you to do the same. In summary, this final Life Lesson is going to be all about you.

I used to have lunch every two weeks with two best friends. One was my brother Harold, and one was Charles Culbertson, a fellow writer. The three of us talked about every possible topic that might come to mind. Politics. Religion. Favorite movies. Favorite books. Favorite authors. Travel to favorite places. Our pastimes and hobbies. Fears. Loves. Disappointments. Family. Other Friends. Enemies. And regrets. The only thing we agreed that was off limits was dishonesty. We were open and trusting with one another, and the food was always good. It turned out to be free therapy for each of us, and we savored those lunch dates like a lonely man hoards old memories.

We came up with a challenge for one another one afternoon. We each agreed to write out the assignment and bring it to the table the next week. This was the title of that assignment:

FIVE PEOPLE WHO,
OR INSTANCES THAT,
HAVE MOLDED MY LIFE
(Without the influences of these people
or these instances, I would be a different person)

At first glance you may think it silly and brush it off. But at second glance, I hope you'll take the challenge, a pencil and paper, and make a list and write a little something about each. Then you can save it or throw it away and never show another living soul. But I promise you, just writing it down for your own enlightenment will be a blessing to you and will make you so aware and appreciative of the people and/or the things you listed that you'll have a smile or a tear before the day is over. I was totally honest and forthcoming and discovered some thoughts and feelings I had never said before, even to myself. It will be cathartic and therapeutic and all that high-thinking stuff, yes, but it will also be just plain out, down-to-the-heart fun!

It will be all about you. Try it and let me know. Don't tell what you wrote, but just tell me what kind of effect it had on you.

1.

2.

3.

4.

5.

Keep your heart with all vigilance, for from it flow the springs of life.

—Proverbs 4:23

About the Author

Don Reid, lead singer for The Statler Brothers, is a three-time Grammy Award-winner with twenty-one gold and platinum albums. He is a member of the Country Music and Gospel Music Halls of Fame. As a songwriter, he holds twenty-one BMI (Broadcast Music Inc.) awards. Also, a television series writer, this is his tenth published book since his retirement from the music industry. Reid lives in his hometown of Staunton, Virginia.